Starting Primary Science

Teaching Matters

General Editors: Sydney Hill and Colin Reid

Starting Primary Science

Edited by
Megan Hayes

Science Inspector, Hereford and Worcester

Edward Arnold

© Edward Arnold (Publishers) Ltd. 1982

First published 1982
by Edward Arnold (Publishers) Ltd.
41 Bedford Square, London WC1B 3DQ

Edward Arnold (Australia) Pty Ltd.
80 Waverley Road, Caulfield East
Victoria 3145, Australia

Reprinted 1985

British Library Cataloguing in Publication Data

Starting primary science.—(Teaching matters)
 1. Science—Study and teaching (Elementary)
 I. Hayes, Megan   II. Series
 372.3'5044   LB1585

ISBN 0-7131-0745-6

All rights reserved. No part of this publication may be reproduced, stored in a retrieval system, or transmitted in any form or by any means, electronic, mechanical, photocopying, recording or otherwise, without the prior permission of Edward Arnold (Publishers) Ltd.

Text set in 10/11 pt Baskerville
Printed by Butler & Tanner Ltd., Frome and London

General Editors' Preface

The books in this series provide information and advice on a wide range of educational issues for teachers who are busy, yet who are concerned to keep abreast of new developments.

The aim is practicality: slim volumes that are sources of authoritative help and swift reference, written and edited by people whose expertise in their field is backed up by experience of the everyday realities of school and classroom. The books are planned to cover well-defined topics relevant to schools in widely differing situations: subject teaching, curriculum development, areas of responsibility within schools, and the relationship of the school to the community. They are published at a time when there is a growing call for increased professional accountability in our primary and secondary schools. The 'in-service between covers' that characterizes these handbooks is designed to contribute to the vitality and development of schools and of the individuals within them.

In this volume, Megan Hayes has assembled a team of contributors who have successfully integrated science into their infant and junior school teaching. They detail their experiences, achievements and disappointments so that all can learn from them. We are given vivid examples of how a teacher who has not trained in science can, with a little care and preparation, introduce the subject to children in a thoroughly absorbing way. Exploring the environment, electricity, animals and even household junk can enrich the normal primary diet by encouraging scientific thinking and analysis from a very early age.

This book will interest those who already teach science in their primary schools, but will be particularly helpful to teachers who through lack of familiarity with the subject, have decided that they are unlikely ever to deal with it. It is one of the authors' main intentions to show just how easily such attitudes can be overcome.

Contributors

Megan Hayes — Science Inspector,
Hereford and Worcester

Mavis Eccles — Headteacher,
Ipsley First School, Redditch

Colin Heath — Headteacher,
Pitmaston Junior School, Worcester

Alex Wall — Teacher,
Abbey Park First School, Pershore

John Devine — Headteacher,
Abbey Park First School, Pershore

Sheila James — Headteacher,
Holmer Infants' School, Hereford

Penny Redshaw — Former teacher,
Holmer Infants' School, Hereford

Contents

1 Introduction   1
Megan Hayes

2 Teaching observational skills   8
Mavis Eccles
Training the different aspects of observational skills   9
Looking at and using things at first hand   9
More precise observations   11
Asking questions about what you can see and then beginning to test your thoughts   15
Looking for and recognizing pattern and stages   17
Measuring and recording observations over a period   18
Soil investigations I   21
Soil investigations II   21
Conclusions   23

3 Science from everyday things   26
Colin Heath
Which is the best washing powder?   27
Investigations of plastics   29
Paper vs. plastic bags   30
Egg boxes   33
Plastic bottles   34
Plastic beakers   36
Plastic cups/non-disposable type   36
String   38
Other similar investigations   39
How warm is a warm place?   39
The technological challenge   41
The spinning top challenge   42
The power bottle challenge   42
Making a bridge   43
Bridge structure II   44
Other challenges   44
Conclusions   45

4 Investigating electric circuits 48
Colin Heath
What is electricity? 48
Apparatus 49
Making a simple circuit 50
Conductors and insulators 53
Using more than one single celled battery 54
Lighting more than one bulb from a battery 56
Switches 58
Further activities 60
Conclusions 61

5 Small mammals in the classroom 64
Alex Wall
Care and management of animals 65
Introducing the animals into the classroom 66
A programme of experiments to study animal behaviour 67
Observation of behaviour 68
Breeding 69
Behavioural characteristics 69
Exploring an empty cage 71
Learning behaviour 72
Using a maze 72
Shape preference 74
Colour preference 76
Left or right orientation 77
Conclusions 78

6 Developing outdoor resources for primary science 82
John Devine
A wild area 82
Trees 83
Tree gardens 84
A weather station 86
Two bee hives 88
The ponds 89
   Planning for a concrete pond 89
   Filling and stocking the pond 93
   The food 'pyramid' 94
Using a pond 95
   Pond-side observations 95
   Pond dipping 95
   Classroom follow-up 95
Conclusions 96

7 Science for younger children — 98
Sheila James and Penny Redshaw

   Structured play — 98
   Ourselves and our senses — 99
   Surroundings — 101
   Interest tables or corners — 102
   Themes and projects — 102
   Feel, touch and texture — 104
   Feet and shoes — 105
   Movement — 108
   Flying, floating and spinning in the air — 110
   Conclusions — 112

References — 115

1

Introduction

Megan Hayes

'I like science because it is interesting ... You can learn about things which you never knew could happen. My best science lesson was when we had tin foil and plasticene and we had to make a boat and see if it would carry some plastic cubes. I made a boat out of Plasticine and it held 24 cubes. The highest amount of cubes held was a hundred and the boat was of tin foil.'

So wrote a child of his enthusiasm for a subject which is by no means an accepted part of every primary school curriculum. However, the case for primary science has been well argued and is by now established. Science was one of the five distinct areas of experience discussed in the 1978 HMI Primary Survey(**1**) along with language and literacy, mathematics, aesthetic and physical education and social studies. No discussion of the present day curriculum of the primary school omits mention of it. The Assessment of Performance Unit(**2**) has reported on achievement in science at age 11 as well as at ages 13 and 15. But still the thought of introducing the subject into the school day is often met with apprehension and lack of understanding.

There are as many ways into primary science as there are styles of teaching. Its very open-ended nature encourages individuality of approach, and it is hoped that this is one of the messages conveyed through the individual style of each chapter in this book. Each is by an experienced practitioner discussing approaches he or she has found to work, ranging from very simple investigations to more sophisticated explorations.

There is the development in depth of the skills of observation which can overflow into unexpected areas of the curriculum. Simple investigations of materials (based on household items) are discussed, fostering awareness of the need to link properties to functions. The fascination of electricity, safely explored, is dealt with. Animals are shown to be of value in the development of attitudes as well as of skills across the curriculum, and the school environment, whatever its nature, is too precious a resource to be ignored. Since certain aims are particular to the teaching of infant age children, the final chapter of the book deals with beginning science in the infant school.

It is probable that there is little new material in primary science yet to be chronicled. It is the method of implementation that forms the discussion point in each of the examples presented. We hope that in reading about the work done in these schools, other teachers will be encouraged to start primary science themselves.

The slowness with which science has been assimilated as an accepted part of the curriculum can only be due to the difficulty of appreciating what is meant by its study at this level. It has been defined as 'a way of understanding the physical and biological world'(HMI Primary Survey). This becomes a more useful statement if the word 'understanding' is explained in greater depth. The sequence in any scientific investigation is the same: *observation*, by as many ways as are relevant, *sorting* into groups with similar properties so that patterns emerge, *prediction* of what will happen under different conditions, *experimentation* to test those predictions and finally, an *explanation* of what happened. To these must be added the skills of measurement and of communication as necessary tools. These are the bones of science at any level. Exploration in this way enables teachers to extend children's skills of language and number, so giving work in these areas a greater relevance. There is within this sequence no reference to age of pupil or to content. Indeed, content is of relative unimportance at this stage. What is important is the situation to which logic is applied and, with children, the conceptual level to which a topic is pursued.

It may be easier to start describing what is meant by science by first concerning ourselves with what is *not* science. Science recollected as studied at secondary school and inappropriately diluted has no place in a primary science curriculum. The copying of notes from encyclopaedias in a neat hand with even neater labelled sketches is not science. Neither is the collection and identification of flowers in season: this may qualify as nature study, but not science unless taken further. Indeed, much of what already takes place in a primary classroom does contain the seed for development into good primary science and may only need recognition as such to form a starting point.

Science in the primary school must be associated with *doing*. From appropriate practical work, discussion will result on what needs to be tried next to find out about the particular part of the environment under study. Whenever a pupil is working at first hand from a real object, be it living or non-living, there is a chance that such work can be developed to include a scientific way of thinking. It is in this way that science is discussed in this book, by drawing on examples of practice in a variety of schools, by teachers working within their own particular styles to satisfy criteria which give a piece of work the stature of scientific investigation.

There are few situations which will not lend themselves to this approach. An example will illustrate.

Every child plays with balls—tennis, ping pong, golf, polystyrene balls, marbles. If each one from a collection is allowed to bounce, they can be sorted into good or bad bouncers and patterns of behaviour become apparent. The concept of a fair test immediately enters. Each ball has to be dropped rather than bounced, and each time from the same height. But what is it dropped onto? Does each bounce equally well from all surfaces—a variety can be tested here, including wood, lino, carpet and felt squares, stone and others. There is no place for judgement by simply *looking* at the balls. Instead it is necessary to plan a sequence of experiments to observe what happens under controlled conditions, to suggest what might happen when those conditions are changed, and to see if the hypothesis was correct. Why materials behave differently might be more difficult to explain but every subject at all levels has boundaries for teacher and taught. Those for science come more readily to mind than many but the remedy exists—teacher and child can find out together.

The point has been made, and with justification, that the scientific approach is already the centre of good primary teaching and that any balanced curriculum will contain its share of observation and comparison though not necessarily with recognizable reference to science in the traditional sense. Indeed, it has been recognized by the Assessment of Performance Unit that the skills implicit in a scientific approach to problems can be taught just as effectively in history, mathematics or social studies or may even be picked up by pupils informally as they play.

Questions of implementation arise when the introduction of science as a 'subject' is considered. How much time should be devoted to it? Should this be specifically slotted into a timetable? Who is to be responsible in the school for its teaching?

Each of these questions must have an answer appropriate to the overall philosophy of the particular school but the solution for each will be based on considerations which apply to all schools. Science at this level is process rather than content based. It is not so much what you investigate but how you approach the problem. Further, other curriculum areas can be considered in this way, even if these are not so practically orientated. It would seem, therefore, that for consistency, it would be best if the work were in the hands of the class teacher. Then a scientific way of thinking can be encouraged generally rather than becoming the approach only for a specific time with a science specialist colleague.

There are two polarized strategies for the inclusion of science. It can be timetabled for the suggested ten per cent of the total working time. Alternatively, science can be drawn out of an existing curriculum as and when the opportunity presents itself. The merit here is that the scientific method can be applied to and permeate the whole of the curriculum and when done well, this provides the best approach. The danger is that it is all too easy for a teacher new to science, without much confidence or expertise, to let the subject get forgotten or neglected. It does require conviction to introduce or emphasize more positively a new dimension in the curriculum. Maybe a compromise is needed and that could be a time when small groups in turn 'do' science, possibly on a topic within the existing scheme of work. This would gradually be extended to all areas until accurate and detailed observation, pattern finding, hypothesizing and testing form almost an intuitive part of the child's thinking. When the problem of introducing science is faced in this gradual way, then what seemed daunting in prospect becomes exciting in practice and the colleague who was hesitant before is infected with the enthusiasm of the child met in the opening paragraph.

The accusation can be made that it is impractical to emphasize the importance of process over content without guidelines. But these do exist. They include published science curriculum material and the checklist by the APU of the concepts on which its testing is based. However, it is true that extent of knowledge is less important than enthusiasm and attitudes. Not infrequently science is encountered at primary level which is little more than half remembered facts from secondary experience, where content has been allowed to take over from process and where the spirit of science has died. Science at the level that we are concerned with is involved with the encouragement of a critical and curious attitude which will serve as the best foundation for the subject orientated science encountered at secondary level.

But all has to be organized, the more particularly because science is a newcomer to the curriculum. In the same way that a school would be expected to have formulated language and mathematics schemes to encourage coordination and progression in those subjects, it is also important that work in science be organized for the school as a whole. The work of coordination could be taken on by the Head, along with the overall responsibility for the curriculum, if the school is small. Alternatively, the responsibility could be allied to that for mathematics as a recognition of the common ground between the two areas. There is an in-service, in-school task of working with colleagues to formulate a scheme for science if it is not only to be paid lip-service.

Schemes can take a variety of forms. Topics across the curriculum can be specific to a particular year and the science component identified. Aspects of the environment, the weather, the flora and fauna of the school grounds, can be treated in increasing depth as conceptual levels develop year by year. Visits to places of interest can be allocated to specific age groups and the appropriate science developed from each. If such details are recorded, then there is order and the risk of repetition is diminished. The marshalling and pooling of ideas that would result if the scheme were brought together by discussion among colleagues could only help everyone to appreciate the aims of having science in the curriculum at this stage.

The materials needed for the teaching of primary science are in the main not elaborate. The tools to put the natural curiosity of children to work are not the traditional tools of the secondary school. Apart from a very few 'set pieces' which would include a stereomicroscope, much overlaps the apparatus recognized as necessary for a good mathematics scheme, such as measuring and weighing instruments and equipment for appreciating volume concepts. Much of what is needed in addition can be thought of as junk. However, it must be organized and assembled in such a way as to encourage use by colleagues. This could be in boxes, each specific to an experiment and with resulting duplication of items. Alternatively, there could be stacks of boxes, each containing a collection of a particular item, ranging from cotton reels to yoghurt pots and kept at a central location. Whatever method is used will depend on the individual school's organization and storage facilities and will be particular to that school. Of paramount importance is that all involved are encouraged to use the equipment.

The responsibility of the coordinator will not be to dictate the approach to be used in teaching science since each teacher has an individual style of working. Rather it will be to help colleagues who have hitherto had their energies fully absorbed in other areas of the curriculum to adopt a new concern that enriches the whole of what went on before its introduction.

The myth that science is only for secondary pupils has been dispelled. The environment is there to be explored, physical as well as biological. Its study in an accessible manner provides too powerful a tool not to be included as an essential part of the educational diet for any child of whatever age.

2
Teaching observational skills

Ipsley First School caters for about 450 children of 5 to 9 years old. Science is taught as an integral part of the whole curriculum and during the school year each class teacher makes sure that science has been the main element of various chosen topics. The Deputy Head has overall responsibility for the subject in the school and she is helped by another member of staff to organize a resource area from which the rest of the staff can borrow apparatus, work cards and books. We try to have a wide selection of materials available, so that there are plenty of ideas for starting points which staff can develop acccording to their class needs.

2

Teaching observational skills

Mavis Eccles

Observation lies at the heart of all work in primary science and it is important to make sure that the skills involved are given every chance to be developed as fully as possible.

Young children before entering school have already used their powers of touch, sight, hearing, taste and smell to discover much about themselves and their environment. In fact, as soon as children notice or experience something new, they have a natural urge to look further to touch, to explore and to ask questions. One should capitalize on this natural quest for discovery, and further the development of the child's natural senses.

We have found that children who have learned how to investigate in a purposeful manner, make sensible deductions, set about devising ways of testing their predictions and constructing a simple hypothesis, have the best start for any later scientific work.

In order to achieve these aims a school environment should be:

   a) *stimulating*, thus encouraging questions and investigations
   b) *well-organized* so that the child learns how to work in an orderly manner
   c) *informative* so that the child can not only be encouraged to seek answers to questions but also so that further queries are raised and
   d) *caring* so that each child has the opportunity to gain enough self-confidence to think and experiment for himself or herself.

In order to ensure progression in the acquisition of scientific skills and concepts it is essential that at all stages the teacher must give the child opportunities to express and record his findings. This feedback provides the only real way in which the teacher can be sure of how much each child has actually gained from an experience. With the younger child the feedback will be in the form of words, open-ended questions being asked by the teacher such as:

   a) What can you see?
   b) Does it always look the same?
   c) Did any changes occur as you watched it?
   d) Why do you think the change happened?

e) Does it look the same wherever you stand?

As the teacher sees or hears what the children have gained, she can then question further to make them look again, she can create tasks or opportunities that enable the children to gain extra practice and thus prepare them for a further stage of development.

Pleasure and satisfaction from work well done are two of the best stimuli for future development and success. This is why it is important that each child's best efforts are used and/or displayed.

The method used to record observational work necessitates careful thought. As the child progresses, the most appropriate form to record in must be consciously decided upon and the choice should be considered, bearing in mind the purpose of the investigation. The various forms of recording are discussed more fully later in this chapter.

Training the different aspects of observational skills

1 Looking at and using things at first hand

This is essential, not only for primary science, but for all aspects of learning. Children need to be able to refer to the real thing whenever possible. It should always be remembered that a picture only gives second-hand information and is very limited in what it can actually tell you. In order fully to understand and interpret a picture, some previous knowledge is almost a pre-requisite. At a later stage pictures and photographs can be very valuable but for the very young child a picture alone cannot give enough information, for it is only a two-dimensional representation of the real thing. For example, a drawing of a leaf, no matter how well done, cannot answer the following questions:

a) Is it smooth or hairy when you touch it?
b) Is it stiff or flexible?
c) Is it fleshy or thin?
d) What colour is it on the other side?
e) Are the veins the same on both sides?
f) Has it a scent?
g) How does it fall to the ground?

The teacher needs to bring things into the classroom so that the children become used to handling and asking questions about objects. The child's finds should be used, too. The utilization of ordinary objects is important so that the child does not grow up thinking that the only things of real interest have to be bought or sought in distant places. A collection of local stones gathered on the way to school, for example, can produce a most interesting source of ideas to follow up. A class of five and six year olds were intrigued by the names given to their different coloured stones and were fascinated to see which kinds were the most porous and which broke easily with a hammer. The teacher brought in lumps of the local stone and soil so that the children could see which of theirs had been carried in from elsewhere.

The immediate environment, no matter where you live, contains limitless starting points for science and should be used in a systematic way by the teacher. If used well the children will then do more than just glance at something. They will begin to make further investigations and will gradually abstract more and more information from what is at hand. If the teacher directs their thoughts with skilful questioning, the children will begin to distinguish quite easily between such general terms as:

> big/little; hot/cold; straight/crooked; wet/dry; living/non-living; heavy/light; hard/soft; rough/smooth; bendy/rigid; solid/liquid; left/right; up/down; in front/behind; tall/short; fat/thin; light/dark; floating/sinking; full/empty; narrow/wide; transparent/opaque; natural/man-made; horizontal/vertical; inside/outside; metallic/non-metallic; same/different; sharp/blunt; pointed/rounded; etc.

The importance of learning terms such as these at first hand cannot be over-emphasized. One of our teachers who was a potter brought into school a collection of pots for her class of five year olds to look at and handle. Many children called the smooth pots 'soft' and the textured pots 'hard'. The children could only learn the differences in the meanings of the words by the close observation and handling of a wide variety of smooth, soft, hard and rough objects together with plenty of adult questioning and discussion. It should always be remembered that young children in particular learn a great deal through touch. Hence their observation takes place through their hands—often mouths if only a baby! Actually, some of this same class needed more help when later they were shown a smooth patterned pot that had been painted. The children who thought it to be rough to the touch had to close their eyes and feel it before they were convinced. Even adults can be surprised at the feel of an object; those who have not felt a snake's skin, for example, often expect it to be slimy.

That care is needed in touching can also be emphasized at this stage. Children respond with great sensitivity to the handling of an egg-shell or a skeleton leaf if its fragility is explained first. Safety ideas can be introduced, too, as the children are made aware of the danger of touching all leaves in case they sting or of the necessity to watch for things that might burn—even ice. One of our six year old boys who was in a wood for the first time searching diligently for feathers, put his hand straight into a bed of nettles. He had not met them previously and was not aware that any plant could hurt.

Teaching observational skills 11

2 More precise observations of why the thing you are looking at is as it is and/or what you can do with it

Some six year old children were looking carefully at the insides of old clocks. They were encouraged to see which parts moved and to see if the movement made anything else happen. Many children drew felt-tip pen pictures of what they could see and this activity, because the teacher constantly questioned them about what joined on where, made them more aware of what was actually there. One of the children,

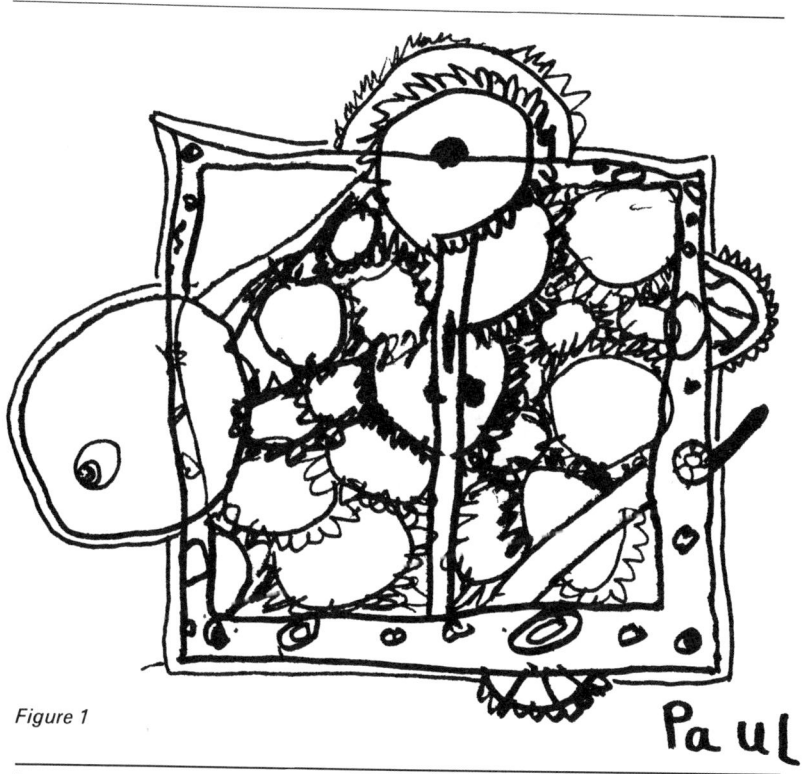

Figure 1

Gareth, then wrote: 'On the machinery there is a cog which you turn round and then another cog goes round on its own. The teeth of the cog are sharp and some are blunt. The number of cogs in this cog is ten. If you turn a cog slowly then a smaller one goes round very fast. A piece of wire looks like a piece of metal, but really it's only wire going fast. The cog which goes round fast is spiky. The cog I moved is blunt.'

At this stage the child needs to be made to concentrate on one thing at a time and to look in real depth. To find out more about a specimen or object the child needs to be taught:

a) to look at it from different angles and levels.
   i) Has it got a top and bottom?
   ii) Do the parts alter as you raise it?
   iii) Is it all in one piece?
b) to look for colours, shades and tints.
   i) Do they stay the same as you walk around it or move it?
   ii) Is the colour important to the object or could it be any colour?
   iii) What happens when a torch is shone on it?
c) to notice the different shapes or parts.
   i) Are they connected to each other?
   ii) Is the connection always in the same way?
   iii) Do some parts look more important than others?
d) to try to establish what it is made of.
   i) Is the same material used throughout?
   ii) Do the textures vary on the different parts?
e) to notice any patterns and how they are arranged.
   i) Is the pattern important to the object?
   ii) If it changes is there any reason for this?
   iii) Can the patterns be seen from a distance?
   iv) Are there certain areas where the patterns would not be easily visible?
f) to use his other senses to help give him extra information.
   i) Touch—it is rough or smooth; do the parts vary; is it the same temperature all over; are there any spiky bits; does it move when you touch it; would it fall heavily to the ground or float down?
   ii) Smell—has it a scent of any kind; if it were possible to crush it would its scent change; how far does its scent travel?
   iii) Taste (with care)—is it bitter or sweet; does the taste remind you of anything?
   iv) Hearing—does it make any sound; what kind of sound; can it hear me?
g) to extend the knowledge gained by his senses through the use of apparatus and tools.
   i) Balances and scales should be available so that the children can use them to discover more about its mass. The different types of weighing apparatus used in mathematics should be at hand so that they can be used as required. As the children progress, they should learn to select the balance best suited for the task.
   ii) Mathematical equipment to enable one to discover more about actual measurements should also be available. Metre

sticks, rulers marked in difficulty according to the age of the child, tape measures, callipers and capacity measures may all be needed at various times.

iii) Thermometers, once again marked in difficulty according to the developmental level of the child, can be used to discover more about temperature. A soil thermometer and a maximum and minimum thermometer are also useful for the older child.

iv) Magnifying glasses, viewers and microscopes. The use of these is very important and they should be introduced from an early age. Young children soon learn how to use a hand lens. It should not be too heavy but should be well balanced and as powerful as one can afford. Care of apparatus and equipment and its correct storage should also be discussed at an early age. Viewers are useful for fragile objects, live specimens, etc. and once again should be as powerful as the school can afford. They should be placed in good light and the class will need to be trained so that individuals can use them as the need arises. Small viewers are useful for group activities and field work.

Great use can be made of the stereomicroscope which does

Figure 2 This was drawn by a six year old with the help of the stereomicroscope.

not need prepared slides. The selection of stereomicroscopes depends upon the layout and resources available to the school. If the school has an area which is accessible to most of the children, then a heavy expensive model may be the best buy as this will be well lit and very powerful. However, in a large school which is spread out, it might be more advantageous to purchase small, cheaper models so that they can be moved easily from room to room. A stereomicroscope is a 'must' for every school.

Magnifying glasses, viewers and the stereomicroscope open up a whole new world for children and make them appreciate that there is more to the structure of everything than meets the eye.

h) to record the information gained in a variety of ways according to the developmental level of the child and to the purpose of the investigation. As the data gained might well be required at a later date, this, too, should be borne in mind so that the easiest means of recall is utilized.

The means of recording used can be in any one or more of the following forms:

1) *Illustration*, where the most suitable art materials for the subject in question can be discussed. Some six year olds on trying out paints, pencil, charcoal, chalk and pastels decided to use chalk to draw the day old chicks they were observing because it was easier to get a fluffy effect. Where the child is trying to show form and pattern, then it is better to limit the colour. We use black fibre tipped pens a lot for this kind of work.

2) *Oral accounts* are important at all ages. Children can relate their finds to a class or group and older children can also learn how to use a tape recorder.

3) *Factual accounts* can be used to encourage the children to write accurately and precisely. They can also be encouraged to think about the arrangment of sentences on the page so that individual facts can be easily retrieved. Headings and underlining can also be incorporated for the older child.

4) *Charts, graphs, plans, tables and maps* can be devised to enable one to add information to a cumulative record. With young children this may well take the form of pictorial representation. For example, the children can easily draw a sun or a cloud or a snowflake according to the weather of the day and then stick it on to the relevant grid so that at the end of two weeks, for example, they can see whether there were more days with sun or rain, etc. These charts or early graphs should become more symbolic as the child develops. The older child should be shown the various ways of recording information such as histograms,

Teaching observational skills 15

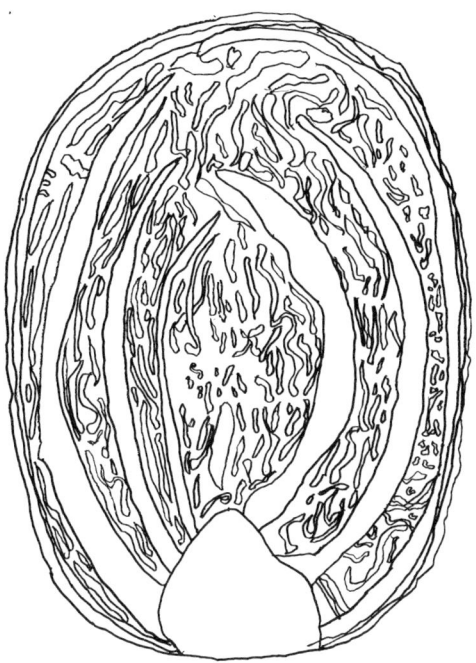

Figure 3 This cross-section of a sprout was drawn with a fibre tipped pen.

pie charts and line graphs to show a trend, diagrams, plans and maps. The same observations recorded in more than one way can be compared to decide upon the merits and disadvantages of each form. It is important, too, that the child is encouraged to predict as the recording develops so that possible conclusions can be arrived at as the work progresses.

It is important that at all stages a child is encouraged to ask questions related to his chart rather than just answering questions asked by the teacher. One has to understand a chart fully to be able to ask a question about it!

3 Asking questions about what you can see and then beginning to test your thoughts

A class of seven and eight year olds were studying the effects of frost and ice as we were suffering a particularly cold spell. They had done some work previously on water. Craig wrote the following from notes he had kept during his day of observation. His comments on how dry flowers can freeze are his own thoughts and were not instigated by the teacher in any way.

Found out on a winter's day
Lee Shrimpton and Lee Kesterton and Kirk Grubb all went outside into the playground because we were doing an experiment. It was snowing. When they came back in we felt their hair and their clothes. Lee Shrimpton's hair felt wet. The ice had probably melted on his head whilst he was outside. Kirk Grubb's hair felt wet and bumpy. Lee Kesterton's clothes felt wet and icy.

I was thinking, how could flowers freeze up when it hasn't been raining? I found out that fog is a kind of steam and steam can be made into water somehow. So if the fog fell onto the flowers it would turn into water and when it got very cold it would freeze.

I am looking over to the School Hall now and on the roof at the very top there is some snow and it looks as if the Hall is touching the sky.

Most things that are cold like snow, ice and many other things turn into water when they have been by a fire. When ice melts and turns into water the water takes less room than the ice.

Each of our tables had a stick that had been cut off a tree. It was covered with frost. About an hour later it was perfectly dry because the ice had melted and the water evaporated.

Yesterday I went out to get some snow for Miss Holt. Yesterday it filled a two litre container. Today there are 400 millilitres of melted snow so snow takes up more room when it hasn't melted than when it has melted.

The teacher concerned then took up several points that Craig and other children had mentioned and developed them with the class.

A group of six and seven year olds were studying a collection of different bricks. Encouraged by the teacher, they considered the texture, shape, size, volume, colour, hardness and density and then made estimations of the mass of each brick by handling. They then compared each of these different aspects by sorting and started to consider why there were differences in the colour, texture, density, etc. After pooling their individual ideas and considering the questions asked by their teacher, they decided that the bricks were each made of a different combination of materials and that perhaps this was intentional because they were probably used for different purposes. They then went on to try to decide what they thought would be the best use for each brick and started by trying to decide which ones would be best for outside walls. Some children soon commented that certain bricks were prettier than others! One child thought that the crumbly brick would be good to include because you could grow a plant in it and make the wall look pretty. This idea was scornfully rejected by the more practical element of the class! This led to discussion on what was needed in an outside wall and the children soon decided that protection from weather was the biggest consideration.

Then, instigated by the teacher, they went on to investigate the porosity of the various bricks by placing each brick upright in water and noting the changes that took place.

This work also developed into:

i) observation of the bricks beneath and above the school damp course.
ii) building with bricks of different sizes and shapes so that the children learned of the importance of uniformity.
iii) observation of the way walls are constructed, how joints are staggered, etc. The children also built walls in different ways and then threw balls at them to observe the results.

An adult came to demonstrate the correct way to build a brick wall and the children handled and learned the correct names of the relevant tools.

4) Looking for and recognizing pattern and stages so that sensible speculation can be aimed for and tested

Children need to be encouraged to watch for and to listen to pattern. They will need to learn how to recognize and repeat pattern in music, mathematics, movement and art work as well as in science, if they are to begin to become skilled in watching for stages which may well be a part of a chain of events. It is important for the child to learn that one observation does not necessarily give the whole answer, and that before conclusions can be arrived at other aspects of evidence may well have to be taken into account.

Some six year olds, when looking at a dandelion plant cut off at the top of the root, had no idea that part of the plant was missing. They thought that the small part of the root that could be seen was the 'holding together bit.' We took the children into the grounds and dug up whole plants. This opened up a whole new dimension for these children and they were then ready to learn about some of the different parts of plants and the use of each component. They could also think about which parts of the plants were absolutely essential for their survival.

Even when the young child is confronted with the full evidence, he or she may well ignore some aspects because they are not able to hold all of the variables in their heads at once. Any conclusions they come to may well be incorrect, but a sensitive teacher, with a knowledge of the developmental level of the children, will know what aspect or aspects to challenge them with so that the children have to reconsider their first conclusions. This should be tackled in such a way that the children do not feel that they have made a mistake, but rather it should show them that any conclusion is subject to change and maybe even total rejection if it does not fit in with new evidence.

At this stage the child can also be encouraged, after careful thought, to speculate on what will happen when the conditions or environment are changed.

After experimenting to find the rate of water flow in a stream, the children thought about what might happen if the flow were interrupted with an obstacle. They then measured any differences when one person stood in the water, then two, then three, etc.

Children looking at bean seeds germinating wondered what would happen if they planted them upside down or on their side and whether the results would be the same in the soil as in a jar with blotting paper. Sensible experiments had to be devised to test their predictions and here the teacher had to step in to point out the need for control experiments.

The value of home-made equipment cannot be over-emphasized. Before children can design a 'machine', they have to think about what they are actually aiming for. The construction of the apparatus often gives them opportunities to start some physical science and its use will usually enable them to see for themselves the need for adaptations to their original designs. Also, when the children come later to use more sophisticated apparatus they will better appreciate the complications of the construction if they have previously worked on making their own.

A teacher needs to be aware of what else a child can do to further his or her investigations. Work cards can be devised to lead the child onto further experiments to find out what happens when a specimen is put in a different situation or environment. For example, what happens when a flower is exposed to sunlight for a week and how does this compare with one left in the dark for the same period? Care, of course, must always be taken with livestock and their conditions should only be changed if they are not going to be hurt in any way. To help the teacher devise suitable oral instructions some of the following starting points may be useful:

> What happens when the subject of the experiment is:
> dropped; bounced; hammered; stretched; bent; immersed in water; heated; dyed; exposed to frost; turned upside down; crushed; dried; and so on.

5) **Measuring and recording observations over a period**

It is important that children are given plenty of opportunities to observe and collect data over a long period so that they learn to look for patterns and relationships. Some five and six year olds kept a simple record of what happened to the oak tree in the playground throughout a school year and then checked their findings during the next year, encouraged by the teacher to try to remember what was likely to happen next.

Work with older children needs to be very carefully planned and carried through so that the children begin to realize the need for systematic and accurate observations and recording. This will provide a good basis for any later scientific work.

The teacher of a class of seven, eight and nine year olds wanted her children to learn something of habitats and ecosystems. Her main aim was to help the children discover and understand that in any area they will find living and non-living things working together, exchanging the materials of life and then using them over again. The work was based on a practical approach.

The class was divided into groups and each given approximately a square metre of the school grounds to study over half a term. The areas included a tree, bush, slope, part of a hedgerow and some rough grass. The children worked in groups but kept individual diaries. The class sometimes worked as a whole when their teacher felt that information needed gathering together or a fresh aspect needed to be introduced. The project covered much more than what would be thought of as pure science and mention is made of some of the other aspects of the curriculum that were touched upon because good observational training and questioning must be going on all day.

After a preliminary talk by the teacher the children went out in small groups to their marked plots taking their note-books, pencils, measures, collecting boxes and a magnifying glass. Discussion took place about the need to conserve and so a flower, for example, was picked only if there were others left. Most of the stones, etc. were also later returned to their original positions. The children had to include in their observations the date and time, notes on the position and size of their habitat, a weather description and something about the conditions of their area on that day. They then had to note details of plants, animals and anything else on the plot. Some of the children's initial notes were very superficial, they just talked of flowers and grass and did not see the need for further identification until it was pointed out by the teacher. Rachel, who was already an observant child, wrote the following but, as you will see, her observations are not yet related to each other in any way.

Date and time. 3.5.1981 at 9.55 a.m.

Situation. I am in the top left-hand corner of the Spinney. It is shady and has about six trees behind. My plot is about one square metre.

Weather. It is quite warm with mixed clouds and a light wind sometimes. There is a bit of humid in the air. (The children had been introduced to the words humid and humidity but they needed a lot of experience and practice before they could use the terms correctly.)

Conditions. Underfoot was very muddy and wet.

Observations. On my plot of land there was a white crisp packet. There were little and big twigs and a piece of bark. The bark was light and dark brown and had a bit of black. I found a broken dog's bone, some dead oak leaves, some dead yellow grass, some green glass, stones, a worm, snail and some grass with opening flowers. The worm was about 10cm long. The snail had a brown and black shell and was 1½cm long. The slug was light and dark brown and was about 3cm long.

On returning to the classroom further work was carried out on the individual finds, and questions were set by the teacher so that the children started thinking about the relationship of one thing to another. When the children had recorded and expanded upon their initial observations, their teacher talked to them generally about ecosystems and they looked at what they had already found to see if they could see any pattern of inter-dependence. They discussed food chains, each person having to draw his or her own food chain sequence, and then built up the diagram shown in Figure 4 so that they could decide where their finds fitted into the cycle. The children illustrated their diagrams to remind themselves of the significance of each part. The teacher had a good selection of reference books at hand from the county library to help supplement information. We sometimes find that certain adult books offer better diagrams and charts than books written specifically for children so these need to be considered, too.

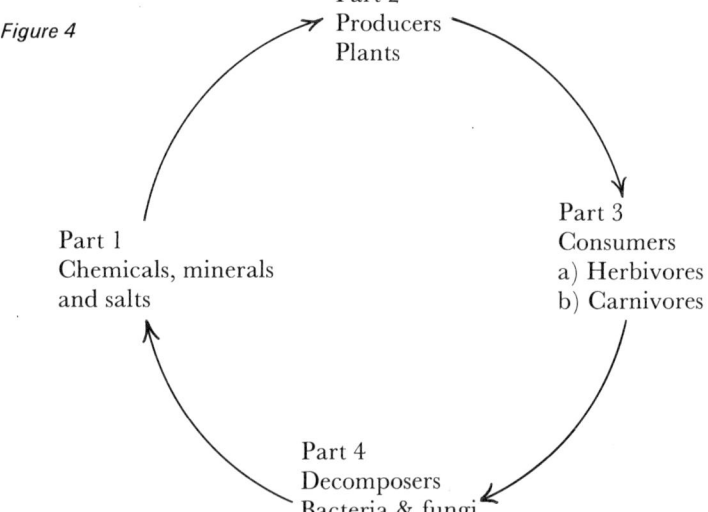

Figure 4

Part 1
Chemicals, minerals and salts

Part 2
Producers
Plants

Part 3
Consumers
a) Herbivores
b) Carnivores

Part 4
Decomposers
Bacteria & fungi

To study a miniature ecosystem the class collected things from a pond including some water, and set up an aquarium in the classroom. By careful observation, using the microscope too, they were able to see some of the inter-reaction of livestock on livestock and livestock on plants, etc. The children were also made to think about their own habitat and they wrote about what was necessary in their individual homes in order to keep each person alive, happy and healthy.

The class made a collection of some of the interesting bits of bark, twigs and stones they had found and started some work on texture using sponges, polystyrene, string and thick and thin paint. They also pressed dried leaves, grasses and some flowers and later made arrangements with them. The magnifying glasses and stereomicroscope were used to help make detailed drawings of some of the specimens. Reference books were used to find out the correct names.

The class then went on to study soil so that they could find out more about their plots. The groups brought approximately one cup full of soil from their plots into the classroom and then progressed through the work-sheets below, which had been previously prepared by their teacher. They worked as individuals and used the dry sand, dry clay and moist clay which was already by the stereomicroscope to answer the questions.

Soil investigations 1

1) Sprinkle a little dry sand on to your investigating paper (about a teaspoonful). Look at it carefully through a magnifying glass. Can you see the individual grains (particles)?
2) Describe the colours in the particles and their shapes.
3) Carefully draw and colour some sand grains. Use the microscope.
4) Rub some sand grains between your fingers and use several words to describe the *texture* of the sand.

Now do exactly the same experiments with the dry clay.
Repeat the experiments with some soil from your plot.

   a) Is the texture of your soil like the sand or more like the clay?
   b) Is the colour of your soil more like the colour of the sand or the colour of the clay?
   c) Can you see sand particles and clay particles in your soil?
   d) Do you think there is more sand in your soil, or more clay? Explain why.
   e) Why do you think different kinds of plants grow in different places?

Soil investigations 2

1) Take a little moist clay and put it on your newspaper. See if you can roll it into a sausage shape.
2) Now take some moist sand and try making a 'sausage' out of this.
3) Repeat your experiments with your soil sample. Write out your experiment under headings:

   a) title
   b) diagram
   c) what we did
   d) what happened

Write down what happened to the three samples when you tried to roll them. Try to explain the differences.
— Is your soil sample more like the clay or the sand when you try to roll it?
— Do you think there is more sand or more clay in your sample?
Rub a little sand, soil and clay on to your writing paper. Describe the colours they make.
— Is your soil more like the clay in colour or more like the sand's colour?

These questions were printed on worksheets but the teacher knew which children she had to watch as they worked through them. Before the class started the work she went through the questions with the class as a whole so that they had some prior knowledge of what was required.

During this whole study there were times when the teacher worked with the class as a whole, the children volunteering information for a class discussion or graph, etc. The less able were helped to contribute, too. At other times the children worked in groups or as individuals, their work being set either orally or on work cards. Two of the least able of this mixed ability class were always dealt with as individuals.

The children did classwork on insects and creatures found in the school grounds. They caught specimens by submerging a jam jar in the ground and leaving it overnight. The children looked up the eating habits of the animals caught and added information to a class chart as shown in Figure 5.

Figure 5

Feed on plants	Feed on animals	Feed on dead things
earwig	centipede	wood lice
aphids	mosquito	worms
snail	dragon-fly larva	etc.

They also thought of man as an omnivore and studied the food they ate in a day and week.

The class carried out experiments to find out more about photosynthesis and learned about chlorophyll and its purpose. A grassed area was covered and observations made daily to see what happened. The growth of selective plants in each plot was also charted and compared.

The children's individual diaries gradually became more detailed as they were now more prepared to poke around and also had more information upon which they could base their observations. Rachel's diary for the beginning of July included the following observations:

> *Observations.* The nettles are now 70cm tall and have some new light green leaves growing up from the bottom. Under some new grass there are decaying things such as dead oak leaves and some rotten

bits of bark which are turning to soil because they are so pulled apart. A piece of decomposing log has an ants' nest in it. There is decomposing yellow grass and dead yellow oak leaves underneath it. I saw a spider's web with lots of white baby flies caught in it and a dead bee. The bee was only 1cm long because something had eaten its body. All that was left were two of its black, furry legs and a bit of its head. The bee had a bit of yellow on it but it was mostly black. Another piece of bark had fungi starting to grow on it. There were some grass flowers, I noticed Common Rye grass and Meadow grass. The dog's bone now has grass growing over it.

Conclusions

Good observational training helps a child develop in all aspects of the curriculum. If taught well the child will:

a) develop more accurate language concepts
b) become more aware of colour and shape
c) be more ready to notice texture, pattern and design
d) be able to deal with more than one variable at a time
e) be more prepared to watch for the inter-reaction of one thing upon another
f) be ready to test and extend his or her findings and so be more accurate in making assessments.

3

Science from everyday things

Pitmaston Junior School caters for approximately 300 children aged 7 to 11 years, and is set in the residential outskirts of Worcester. Science is taught to all classes usually by the class teacher, and may be integrated with other aspects of the curriculum. Some topics are science based while in others the science element is complementary to environmental or geographical aspects. Each class spends the equivalent of 1 to $1\frac{1}{2}$ hours per week on science spread throughout the year.

3

Science from everyday things

Colin Heath

Science is all around us, and is part of our everyday lives. Almost everything we meet illustrates some scientific idea or principle. Therefore one important aspect of science in the primary school is that of children initiating and devising experiments using everyday things. However, for the non-specialist teacher this can, in prospect, be a very daunting approach because it requires, in the initial stages, sailing into uncharted waters. Nevertheless, this can be so stimulating and enjoyable for the teacher and children alike that it is well worth taking the plunge.

A common remark made by teachers inexperienced in primary science is that they do not know the answers to their investigations and are concerned about revealing to the children their own lack of knowledge. Although this can be a very real worry it can also lead to a chicken and egg situation. In primary science, as has been seen in the previous chapter, we are far more concerned with the methods of enquiry and the practice of skills than with a list of 'facts' to be learned.

In most of the experiments suggested in this chapter there are no real 'facts' or answers and therefore the teacher need not worry about knowing the answers. Indeed, preconceived ideas can be a positive disadvantage at times.

The main skills required are those employed everyday in the primary school—those of stimulating the children to consider a problem carefully and to suggest fair ways of discovering the answer. In PE, for example, a teacher does not need to know all the different ways a child can use his or her body to make a bridge shape before setting the task. In fact, one of the pleasures is observing the ingenuity of some children—and not necessarily the most intelligent or conformist. In time the teacher and the class build up an understanding of what is required and develop attitudes of approach which can result in undreamed of levels of achievement.

How then can one set about trying this approach?

One way is to introduce such a series of investigations by talking about TV advertisements and how manufacturers try to persuade potential customers that their product is the best on the market. This can lead to discussion on the need to make comparisons of the various brands of a product. Here a few words about the Consumers' Association and *Which* magazine might be of value. Could we, as a class, form our own *Which* testing laboratory?

Which is the best washing powder?

What about the question, 'Which is the best washing powder?' This is a very vague question that needs to be tidied up before fruitful investigations can come from it.

> Best for what? For automatic washing machines, for twin tubs or hand washing?
> Best for all clothes, all colours, all fabrics?
> Best for slightly soiled or very dirty clothes?

Since a washing machine is not a normal piece of equipment in most primary schools, any suggestions about how tests may be carried out must involve less sophisticated equipment.

What can we carry out tests upon? Discussion should lead to the need for a standard test piece which is of the same fabric, colour, size and degree of soiling. It is far better to go for the dramatic illustration, e.g. simulated muddy white football shorts, rather than the slightly soiled handkerchief.

Another question to be considered is, 'Which washing powders shall we test?' Ask the children which washing powder their family uses and they will no doubt tell you why and what their parents think of the other brands! Initially it is better to restrict the number and type of washing powders to be tested to about six, thereby making the investigation manageable and perhaps leaving scope for further tests.

Having decided on the type of fabric, level of soiling and washing powders, thought should be given as to how the tests may be carried out. A method used successfully with classes of children in the 8 to 10 year age group started with introduction to the topic followed by a discussion of the questions raised above. The washing powders to be tested were then decided upon and arrangements were made for children to bring samples from home. The class was then divided into six groups.

A suitable white cotton sheet was produced and divided into seven pieces approximately 30cm square. Each piece was marked with a number in the top corner, using a laundry marker. A visit to the playing field soon effected the soiling of the samples which were left to dry naturally in the classroom. The seventh sample was kept as a comparison.

After discussion, it was decided that washing by hand was liable to produce too many variables involving things like how vigorously the samples were rubbed and how much water was used. Therefore, our own version of a washing machine was decided upon. The 'drum' would be a standard 200g coffee jar with screw-on top—an item held in stock in the 'useful junk collection.'

Each sample would be washed in a half litre of warm water (50°C). It was decided that 5 grammes of washing powder would be used. Agitation would be by inverting the jar 200 times at the same speed. Rinsing would be done in cold water from the tap with 50 agitations. Two rinses were considered adequate.

The methods having been decided upon and everything prepared for the next day when the tests were to be carried out, the children went happily home to obtain the necessary washing powder samples.

The next morning the children arrived enthusiastically, some clutching their labelled samples of washing powder, and as the weather was cloudy and promising rain a washing line was stretched across the classroom. The samples to be washed were distributed to the groups and a list made of which washing powder was to be used on each sample. Although the children would have preferred to spend considerable time obtaining water at exactly 50°C by mixing quantities of hot and cold water I decided that, for expediency, we would use the hot water from the cloakroom tap which was at 45°C. During the washing process many unexpected observations were made. (The powder was dissolved before the samples to be washed were put in.) Some powders dissolved quickly while others took considerable time. The 'speckles' of blue seemed to create considerable interest and many children were amazed to notice that some powders seemed to make the water appear dirty before washing commenced! One child suggested this was deliberate policy by the manufacturer, as it gave the impression that the powder removed more dirt than it actually did. I wish I had taken my camera to photograph the faces of the children as the agitation of the coffee jar washing machines took place. It was a picture of deep concentration and attention.

At the end of the washing cycle, notes were made about the appearance of the water and the amount of lather produced. When all the jars had been inspected we proceeded to the rinsing stage. Half a litre of cold water was taken straight from the tap and the washing was given 50 agitations. Two such rinses were considered adequate. This was soon done and there was a keen interest in the removal and opening out of the samples.

It was agreed that although all the samples were quite clean none would have passed the 'window test', but we decided that, to be fair, much hotter water should have been used. Each sample was then carefully hung up to dry.

When the samples were dry, each child examined them and gave a mark out of ten for cleanliness. The marks were then averaged and we arrived at an order of merit.

On other occasions, it has not been revealed to the children which samples were used with each powder but instead the identification numbers were covered up and each was given a letter. There are some children whose loyalty to their group or parent's brand causes them to be less than objective in their assessment.

This experiment which can be done by a large group of children, as all the materials are readily available, utilizes a number of skills which may be employed at the appropriate level for the class, and illustrates very well the concept of making a fair test. The children can employ the skills of measurement of length (size of sample), capacity (water), weight (washing powder) and temperature in a realistic way.

Further work could be done on the cost per unit (5g) of each washing powder and compared with the test results.

Other observations which the children may make are: How long does it take each powder to dissolve? Does the powder alone impart any colour to the water? How much lather is produced? How long does it last? Is the amount of lather related to the effectiveness of the powder? How well does the powder rinse out? Does the final dry sample have a good 'feel' to it or is it hard, soapy, etc? Is there a smell left behind which everyone agrees is pleasant or unpleasant?

There is much scope for further discussion and enquiry on aspects which can be investigated objectively. Some, of course, are a matter of subjective opinion and it is useful that the children meet them.

Further experiments could compare low lather and traditional powders of the same and different brands or the effectiveness of biological powders with and without soaking. The extensions are endless. It is essential that the teacher has in mind some ideas about how the investigations may proceed. This does not mean that these ideas are imposed on the class. In fact, it is essential to guide the children through a problem by using their suggestions, stimulating them to consider carefully and tidy up their thoughts in order that a course of action can be decided upon.

Although I have carried out this series of experiments with children in the 8–10 age group, this does not mean that it cannot be carried out with other age groups including children in the infant school. The only real changes would be in the degree of accuracy of the various measurements employed.

Investigations of plastics

Investigating the properties of plastic items and packaging materials can be most fruitful and there is certainly no shortage of readily available material for testing. There are many items that, until recently, have been made with natural materials and which are now increasingly made from various types of plastic. Are these changes for the better?

Which are better: paper or plastic bags; pulp board or plastic egg boxes; glass or plastic bottles; card or plastic disposable beakers; pottery or plastic beakers; cotton or plastic string? This looks like another job for your own class *Which* testing team.

How the class is organized will depend upon the teacher and experience of the children. Either the whole class working in pairs could tackle one aspect at a time, or the whole class could be split into groups of six or eight children and each group tackle one aspect. Within the groups, each child works with a partner but may discuss the methods employed and the findings with the whole group. In this type of investigation, it will not be sufficient for the teacher to distribute materials and workcards and set the children working, for many may well be clueless about how to proceed.

Many science workcards are written with a carefully structured list of questions and activities which, if followed methodically, will lead to a set result or conclusion. However, there are occasions when the onus for designing the experiment should be put on the children. In the investigations of plastics described in this section, the thought and discussion are more important than the findings.

An example of this approach is the investigation of paper and plastic bags.

Paper vs plastic bags

Children are very familiar with both paper and plastic bags of the type used to wrap purchases from shops. Have they ever considered why paper bags are used on some occasions and plastic ones on others? Do each have advantages and disadvantages?

The questions could be introduced by showing the children a collection of small bags of several types and asking them to suggest reasons why a particular bag is used. A list of the uses for each type could be built up on the blackboard from the children's suggestions. A typical list might read:

Paper Bags	*Plastic Bags*
fresh fruit	fruit and vegetables
loose sweets	dried fruit
cakes and bread	wet fish
fabrics, cotton thread, etc.	meats (raw and cooked), sausages, etc.
small items from the hardware shop	sandwiches
household items	nails and screws

It is apparent from the above list (and from the fact that many supermarkets only use plastic bags) that although one type may be better for some items, there is no hard and fast rule.

Comparisons can be made between various properties of the two basic types. For this I provide about six samples of both types for each pair of children. Ask the class:

a) How can we compare the strength of each type of bag? What do we mean by strength? How can we test resistance to tearing?

There are various ways of testing, and only if no suitable suggestions come from the children should the teacher offer any, e.g.:

i) Roll the bag in the form of a Christmas cracker and pull apart. Although the result of this test will be rather subjective, many brown paper bags of the type used by greengrocers are so strong that many children cannot tear them in this form!

ii) Hold one side of the open end of the bag and from the other side suspend weights until the bag tears.

iii) Cut strips from the bag to form loops which again may have weights suspended from them.

iv) Hook a piece of stout wire through the centre of the bag and suspend weights from it. How much weight may be supported before the bag tears? Examine the bag where it has torn. Has it torn evenly or not? Did it stretch before tearing? How much? Did it tear suddenly or slowly?

b) Compare the bags' abilities to hold various substances.

The objects used will depend on what is available, but heavy items will test some bags to destruction, which gives a positive result. Both damp and dry sand provide interesting results. Damp sand tends to weaken paper bags and causes them to burst after a few minutes, while dry sand may reveal any gaps in the seams. Sharp, hard objects like nails or screws, pencils or modelling tools, tear paper bags easily, whereas plastic bags tend to stretch and puncture rather than tear.

Heavy objects like iron masses (i.e. weights), usually put too much strain on the bags and the maximum weight held provides an interesting statistic. Where the bag is supported while the objects are put into it, is of great importance here. The length of time a paper bag will hold water before springing a leak adds a new dimension to the measurements taken in this activity.

c) The ease of fastening a bag containing a reasonable amount of sand or sawdust is an interesting comparison.

Watching a shop assistant twisting the corners of paper bags by swinging their contents over and over has probably fascinated many children. How effective a method is this? How well closed is the bag? Is the strength of the top corners increased by this twisting? Is there a minimum and maximum number of twists? What happens when this method is used on plastic bags? Why? What alternative methods of closing such bags are used? What are the advantages and disadvantages?

d) Comparing the strength 1) by blowing up and bursting; 2) by dropping in weights.

Children love to explode bags by blowing them up and hitting them with the hand. This method, of course, can only give a subjective assessment of how easy or difficult it is to destroy them. Plastic bags are too strong or elastic to be burst by this method, whereas most paper ones will submit. What sort of blow from the hand is required? What happens when the bag is squeezed rather than hit? How and where the split occurs could prove of interest—in the middle, where it was hit, at the seam, etc. Observant children may notice the springiness of the air inside the bag and comment on it. This could lead to investigations on balloons, bicycle tyres and inflated balls. Although enterprising children have tried blowing up bags using a bicycle pump and a valve, none has managed to obtain an airtight seal and succeed!

When comparing the relative strengths by dropping in weights, it is of course necessary to drop the weights from the same height each time. More and more weights can be dropped in until the bag tears. Alternatively, the height a single weight is dropped from may gradually be increased by, for example, 5cm, until the bag gives way. Where and how the bag is held is again crucial.

e) Compare the joints or seams of the bags.

How are they made? On paper bags is there the same amount of overlap at the seam on the bottom as at the side? Is there a reason for this? Is the side seam exactly at the edge or not? Is there a reason? Is the glue used waterproof or water soluble? Any reasons? How is the plastic bag joined? Are the seams even or not? Is there an overlap? Are there any weaknesses along them? Cut a strip 2cm wide horizontally along the bag to form a loop. Hang weights on it. Is the seam the weakest part?

f) Compare sandwiches and fresh fruit kept in bags for a period of several days.

What changes do you notice each day? We often say fruit and vegetables 'sweat' in plastic bags. Is this a good description? Where does the moisture come from? Does the addition of holes in a plastic bag increase the length of time fruit may be kept fresh in it? Why are plastic bags of this type used by supermarkets in favour of paper bags? Where does the fruit begin to decay?

g) Can you measure the thickness of the bags?

This can pose quite a problem and it depends on the age of the children as to what degree of accuracy can be obtained. The most satisfactory ways are:
i) to measure a pile of 10, 20 or even 50 bags and divide the answer by twice the number (each bag has two sides).
ii) to measure how many bags are required to make a pile 5mm high and again divide. Plastic bags are usually much thinner than paper ones.

A more accurate measurement can be obtained using a simple micrometer on a number of bags but only top junior age children can really manage this.

The teacher's task, having posed the questions and set the children working, is to go round the groups checking on progress, asking pertinent questions, prompting other lines of enquiry and generally encouraging discussion and thought.

Recording of results and findings will depend on the age and ability of the children. I have carried out tests on bags with children from 6 to 11 years and all have found it a fascinating series of investigations.

The very young children produced good captioned drawings, and bar charts of some of the results were constructed. Lower junior age children (8+) are able to write fully about their investigations and findings, including false leads, and say what they propose for further work. (It is important to encourage children to record their false leads as well as successful investigations.) Top junior age children (11+) are able to be quite precise in their measurements, draw very interesting graphs of the results, analyse them and record fully their observations.

Egg boxes

The various types of egg box currently used by supermarkets and shops can be investigated in a similar manner to the bags. The types used locally are: pulp boxes (at least two designs), expanded polystyrene (made from expanded granules like ceiling tiles), and vacuum moulded polystyrene boxes which are transparent, hard and brittle. Each has advantages and disadvantages.

The children could begin by making a visual examination of the various types and suggesting some advantages and disadvantages of each. Questions to consider could include: is the method of fastening the box a good one? How easily can it be opened when full of eggs? Do the weights of the types of boxes differ significantly? Is the weight of the box a consideration in transporation and handling costs? (One enterprising group calculated that the additional weight of pulp boxes over expanded polystyrene ones would amount to about $\frac{1}{2}$ tonne on a lorry load of eggs!)

The most fascinating investigation, however, is raised by the question, 'How well does each type of box protect the eggs?' Here, as in many other investigations with plastics, testing to destruction is necessary and of course very popular! Plasticine moulded into the shape of an egg is very good as it will reveal where the weakness of the box has allowed pressure to be put on the contents during the tests.

Tests carried out by children into relative strength have involved dropping the boxes containing Plasticine eggs from various heights and observing the results and piling weights or heavy objects onto the boxes until they collapsed. There are, of course, many discussion points for the investigators. How should the weights be placed on a box? Should they be piled high on one corner or spread evenly over the whole box? Should a piece of rigid hardboard, or similar material, be placed on top of the box first to distribute the weight evenly? Discussions among children about this type of question while they are working are essential and should be encouraged.

The effect of a broken egg or water on the strength of the boxes is also an interesting point to consider.

The whole topic could be rounded off by asking the children to design a better egg box themselves, perhaps, with the advantages of the best type and none of the disadvantages.

Plastic bottles

'Have you noticed the introduction of a number of different new designs for plastic bottles recently?' This can be the subject of yet another series of investigations for the *Which* team. The bottles we have tested fall into three main groups. Those used for:

   a) harmful or dangerous liquids, e.g. bleach.
   b) messy but relatively harmless liquids, e.g. squash or cooking oil.
   c) liquids under pressure, e.g. fizzy drinks.

It is in the design of the bottles used for *c*) that the most recent advances have been made.

There are many different combinations of bottle type which may be investigated, but I think it is probably best to limit each group of children to two or three types at one time, otherwise there is a danger of superficiality in their work.

A comparison of one bottle from each of the three groups is one possibility. Here the questions may be: how suitable is each bottle for its intended purpose and what disadvantages would there be if it were used for a different purpose? For example, if the squash bottle were used for cola or bleach?

The tests should simulate the sort of 'accidents' which may happen in a shop or the home, e.g. dropping from various heights, full and partly full; rubbing on an abrasive surface; dropping weighty objects on the bottle from various heights, etc. Matters of safety are also important and the children could discuss where bleach should be stored at home and at what height it should be displayed on supermarket shelves.

A comparison of the bottle types used for fizzy drinks links very well with work on structures and forces, as the designs must withstand pressure from within, which is an interesting aspect in itself.

Whether glass and plastic bottles should be compared in the same way is a question I have always answered negatively because there is no

Science from everyday things 35

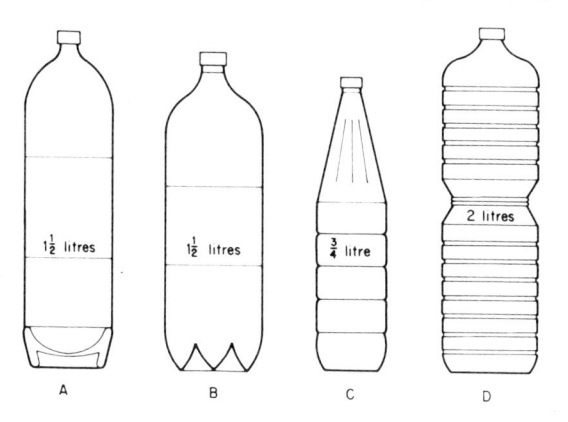

Figure 6a **Soft Drink Bottles**

Type A: Lemonade bottle. Transparent hard bottle body with hemispherical bottom. Top and bottom are white semi-translucent polythene. Capacity—1½ litres.

Type B: Lemonade bottle. Hard transparent plastic body (clear) with five domed base. Metal cap. Capacity—1½ litres.

Type C: Squash bottle. Semi-transparent plastic. Metal screw-cap. Capacity—¾ litre.

Type D: Squash bottle. Clear transparent plastic with horizontal ridges. White plastic push-on cap. Capacity—2 litres.

Figure 6b Household Plastic Bottles

Type A: Domestos. Blue opaque, waisted and fluted. Red plastic screw top.

Type B: Comfort. Turquoise opaque plastic. White screw top.

Type C: Squash. Translucent plastic. White screw top.

Type D: Stergene. Light blue opaque plastic. Yellow plastic screw top.

completely safe way to do it. The children are well aware of the problems of the breakage of glass bottles without smashing any at school!

Plastic beakers

If you buy drinks from vending machines or at fêtes, etc. you have probably noticed that there are various types of disposable cups in use. Why not investigate the advantages and disadvantages of each type, i.e. the waxed card cup, heat moulded plastic cup and expanded polystyrene cup? Questions that need asking are:

Look at each type of cup carefully. What are they made from? Can you tell how they were made? Are there any probable areas of weakness as a result of the method of manufacture? How can you test your theories?

Are the cups usually used for different purposes? How good are they for this purpose? Do the cups, usually used for hot drinks, keep the contents hot while not transmitting too much heat to the fingers when they are picked up?

Can you make up a way of testing their strength—sideways and downwards? How stable are they? Are they easily knocked over when full, half full, or empty? Can you suggest any improvements in the design of disposable cups?

Most means of investigation of the above aspects will be similar to those described for the egg boxes and so they will not be repeated here. Obviously, though, close supervision must be exercised over children using hot (not boiling) water for investigations, although this is within reasonable limits for juniors aged 10+. (I have found the *Thermostik* thermometer manufactured by Osmiroid a reasonably accurate and very robust thermometer in the hands of children.)

Plastic cup/beakers—non-disposable type
Although I have not allowed children to test the non-disposable type of beaker to destruction, because of the wide variety of designs they can nevertheless form the basis of a very interesting investigation. The types we have studied are:

i) those of the type used by the school meals service for water
ii) those produced for very young children, i.e. baby cups
iii) those made for use on picnics, etc.

Most of the investigations children in my charge have carried out have been into stability, although there are other possible investigations. It is a salutary lesson that children who are quite familiar with measuring and drawing angles in the course of their mathematics work are often unable to apply the same skill to an investigation in science.

The two methods we have used, although by no means the only ones possible, are as follows:

i) The swinging weight method
This was by far the most popular and least difficult method.

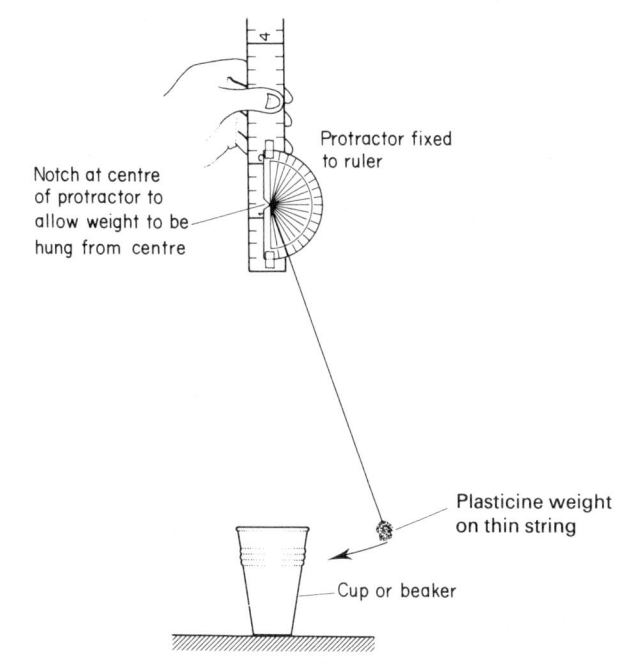

Figure 7   Testing the stability of plastic cups.

The weight was made from 5g of Plasticine which was attached to a piece of string about 40cm long. It was necessary to cut a notch in an ordinary school protractor in order that the string could be fixed at the centre of the circle. The protractor was fixed to an old ruler with Blutack for simplicity. If you have a retort stand to use, this allows the height of the bob to be adjusted easily, so that the beaker or cup under examination may be struck at different positions. The bob is drawn back to angles of 5°, 10°, 15°, 20°, and so on before being released, until it knocks the beaker over. We found that the results obtained when a liquid like water was used as the contents differed from when a less messy substance like dry sand was used, although both produced interesting results.

ii) Tilting test
In this method the beaker was placed on a sheet of hardboard which could be tilted more and more until the beaker fell over. The board was placed near the edge of the table which made it possible to measure the angles without adapting the protractor.

One disadvantage of this method is that the beaker tends to slide rather than fall when the board is tilted and, although this can be prevented by placing it by a barrier made from a strip of card or Plasticine, it is open to question whether this affects the results significantly. However, as the conditions will be the same for each beaker under investigation, it is unimportant. Care must be taken to ensure the board is not wet as surface tension may hold the beaker in place and invalidate the results!

String

Why ponder the age-old question of 'how long is a piece of string?', when it would be more interesting to spend your time examining how different strings are made and comparing their strengths?

Many of the synthetic strings are made in a totally different way from the traditional cotton and sisal ones and it is not difficult to collect or purchase quite a range of thicknesses and types.

Initially this investigation can be carried out by the children individually. Each child is given a short length, say 15cm of the samples of string and asked to undo them, noting how they were made. This should reveal that some synthetics are made from a thin ribbon which has been folded, while others have been plaited rather like the natural fibre ones. The main difference in these latter two types is that the synthetic ones are made from continuous filament fibres while the natural fibres have a variety of staple lengths. A hand lens or ideally, a stereomicroscope, greatly enhances these observations. These initial investigations should reveal a number of aspects which are worth further examination:

How many plies, if any, has the string? Does plaiting or twisting the string in manufacture add strength to it? Are the three or nine plies together stronger than the total strength of the individual plies? How resistant are the strings to fraying at the ends? How resistant are they to abrasion? Can reasonable abrasion tests be carried out by putting the string under tension and rubbing with an abrasive material like sandpaper or a piece of brick? What is the effect of water on the various strings?

Care must be taken in choosing reasonably safe methods of testing breaking strains, since some synthetic strings are extremely strong. A method I have used without mishap is to suspend a builder's bucket by the string from a girder or similar rigid structure near the ceiling, so that the bucket is about 10 to 15cm from the floor. Weight in the form of bricks or damp sand, is then added to the bucket until the string breaks. The breaking strain is then calculated. It is interesting to observe whether or not the string breaks more often in a certain place, e.g. near a knot.

Other similar investigations

There are a number of other inquiries of a similar nature which may be carried out either as an alternative to those mentioned, or in addition to them. It very much depends on what material is available at the time. Food trays of the type used by supermarkets for holding meat and vegetables under cling film can be examined in a similar way to egg boxes.

Have you ever thought of comparing plastic and steel teaspoons, or cutlery in general?

If you have any budding 'Percy Throwers' in your class, an investigation into the various types of plant pot could provide more than just subjective opinion regarding the advantages and disadvantages of each.

What about the different designs of yoghurt tubs or margarine tubs? Are they merely brand identification symbols or do some have structural advantages?

In the area of craftwork, there is the comparison of natural balsa wood and synthetic Balsalite or natural timber with Contiboard and Contiplas.

Then there is the investigation of pure wool knitting yarn and the various synthetics—nylon, Acrilan, Orlon, etc., in addition to the mixtures of each. Sewing threads can also be examined in the same way, not to mention the fabrics themselves.

All these investigations may be carried out by all children in the primary age range with varying levels of accuracy and teacher supervision.

How warm is a warm place?

In those distant days when school milk was provided for junior age children, I periodically arranged for the children to make butter from the cream on their milk. This was a fascinating class activity with everyone taking a turn in shaking the churn (a large screw-top coffee jar) and of course everyone had to taste the result spread on bread or cream crackers—even those who said they did not like butter! Eventually I began to consider whether we could make our own bread. We did this with the cooperation of the school cook or at times the caretaker's wife. However, my class became interested in the statement in the recipe, 'place the dough in a warm place until it has doubled in size'.

Someone raised the obvious question, 'How warm is a warm place?'. As I had at that time a class of top junior children (11 + years), I decided that we could investigate the question with some degree of sophistication.

The first thing we examined was the yeast itself. As I was unable to find at short notice a supply of fresh yeast, we used dried yeast. Information culled from various sources provided the children with clues on how to begin their investigations:

Yeast is a tiny living plant which is found everywhere in the world except for deserts and oceans. It can be found on decaying fruits, trees and even on insects. It is a dependent plant and needs sugar dissolved in water in order to live. It is used for making bread, wine and beer. In feeding, it digests sugar thereby producing carbon dioxide and alcohol as wastes. When conditions are unfavourable the yeast plant goes into a resting stage and produces tiny spores. These spores are rather like seeds, although they are not seeds because they do not contain a store of food. When conditions become favourable again, that is when moisture, sugar and warmth are available, the yeast spores grow into yeast plants.

Having examined the dried yeast through a hand lens, the children set about using the above information to try to 'bring the yeast back to life'.

This they did by putting about $\frac{1}{2}$ gramme each of dried yeast and sugar in a test tube half filled with warm water (approximately 40°C) and shaking it. In order to maintain an even temperature, the test tube was stood in a beaker or jar, half filled with water at the same temperature. There was great excitement when after about 10 minutes bubbles began appearing in the brown liquid. A control experiment of a test tube containing only sugar and water suggested that the yeast was responsible for producing bubbles. This raised two more questions—what were the bubbles and how could we collect some of them for testing?

There are times in learning through discovery when it is necessary to provide information for the children in order that they may proceed with their investigations. I therefore decided to help them by mentioning carbon dioxide, which many knew was present in exhaled breath, and telling them how to carry out a lime water test on their breath by blowing gently into the lime water through a drinking straw. (If you are unable to make lime water, you can usually get some from the science department of your local secondary school.)

We then said that if the yeast was 'breathing', it was possible that the gas produced by it was carbon dioxide. The next problem was how to catch and collect the 'mystery gas'. In view of the age of the children I decided to show them how to collect a gas under water (*Figure 8*).

When a test tube of the gas had been collected, one child put a thumb over the end of the tube before taking it out of the water. Then a small amount of lime water was poured into the test tube and it turned milky immediately. (*Note:* If the test tube is shaken very much you may find that the lime water turns milky and then becomes clear again.)

We were then ready to investigate the 'warm place' aspect of the bread recipe.

Test tubes of yeast and sugar water at different temperatures were set up and the amount of carbon dioxide produced in a given time was measured. Graphing the results showed clearly that there was an opti-

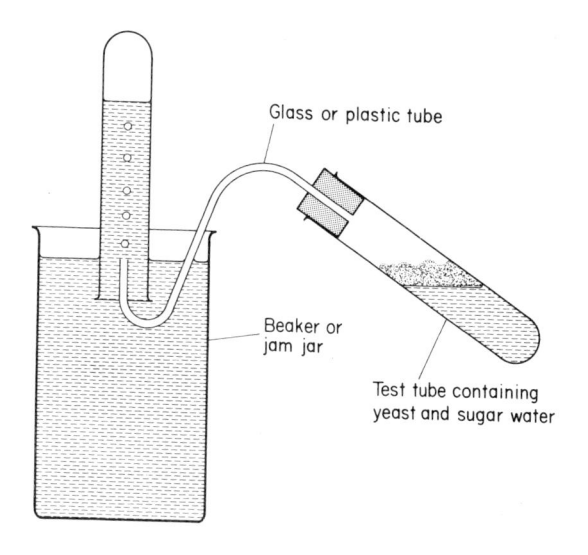

Figure 8 Collecting carbon dioxide gas.

mum temperature for yeast activity and that if it was too hot or too cold, fewer bubbles were produced. Needless to say we made some more bread after our yeast investigations and were pleased with the rise of our dough and the better texture of the bread. We also amended our recipe to read 'very warm place'. What temperature is that? Well, why not investigate for yourself!

The technological challenge

Have you ever noticed that when you issue a challenge to children they cannot resist it? This is a very good method of stimulating interest in sometimes fairly simple ideas which have important scientific principles behind them. Children are quite familiar with the effects of friction, inertia and energy as they meet them in their daily lives. Every child knows how difficult it is to set in motion a fairly heavy wheeled object and yet how much easier it is to keep it moving. Just look at their faces when they start off on their cycles! At an even younger age they discover that they cannot 'stop dead' when running, and until they come to terms with this scientific principle tend to crash into things.

A child trying to run across an icy playground is certainly made aware of the principle of friction. Therefore, although primary age children are not ready to deal with these principles theoretically, they can extend their knowledge by carrying out investigations.

The spinning top challenge

The spinning top challenge is a very straightforward challenge/investigation into the principles of inertia and friction. The children are challenged to make the best spinning top possible from a piece of thin card and a match-stick. If the children are able to use compasses to draw circles (and with the advent of the new, safe, Triman type, even young children are able to do so), that is all the skill they need. Circles of different diameters are drawn on a standard thickness card and a hole made at the centre. A match-stick is then pushed carefully throught the hole and the top is complete. By varying the diameter of the circle of card and the length of match-stick above and below the card, a very effective design can be arrived at. Questions to be considered by the whole group include:

1) How can the best top be judged? E.g., will it be the longest spin from several trials or will it be the average of three or five trials?
2) How will the length of spinning time be measured?
3) What is the best surface for the trials to take place on? Schools with laminated plastic topped tables are more fortunate here than those still using the traditional desks.

When the children have explored the possibilities of a single piece of card and match-stick other variables may be introduced if the children have not suggested them. Obvious ones are:

    a) What is the effect of making a point on the spinning end of the match-stick?
    b) What is the effect of using two or more card circles joined together?
    c) What is the effect of adding weight to the card by placing small pieces of Blutack or Plasticine equidistant round the edges?
    d) What is the effect of spinning the top on different surfaces? etc.

The results of their researches into all these questions will lead to the optimum dimensions and shape of the spinning top. In arriving at this arrangement the children will have met and explored the scientific principles of inertia and friction which govern so much of our movement whether as individuals or in various machines.

The power bottle challenge

Our power bottle challenge was probably the most successful project we have undertaken. It stemmed from a school project on the theme of bottles and generated considerable interest from the children and their parents. Each child was given a copy of the rules and a standard rubber band. They were asked to use the elastic band to propel a standard size (540ml) washing-up liquid bottle further than anyone else, along a measured course in the school hall. There was no restriction on help from parents on this occasion, since the children made their models at home and I wanted to stimulate parental involvement in the project. Many designs were tried out and some very sophisticated machines were brought to school for the initial trials. I did, incidentally, make a machine based on the principle of the schoolboy cotton-reel tank which I allowed the children to examine. In the copy of the rules for the competition, it was pointed out that the rubber band was a device for storing energy which could be released slowly to propel the bottle. There were no restrictions on how the band was to be used and experiments were made into the effect of cutting the band in two lengthwise and making it into a ribbon. The frictional resistance at the point where the bottle or its driving wheels touched the floor had to be varied until the optimum level was obtained. The question of lubrication of any bearings was solved most successfully, to the surprise of many, by using not oil, but washing up liquid! The trials and heats were held and excitement was high for the finals.

The winning machine was made by an 8 year old boy much to the good-hearted disgust of the self appointed engineers in the fourth year! This machine consisted of a washing-up liquid bottle to which driving wheels made from polystyrene ceiling tiles had been added. The 75mm × 7mm rubber band drove the machine 55 metres in the finals, although greater distances had been achieved in practice. Can your children beat that?

Making a bridge

Children often discover in the course of their early play some very important scientific principles which, although they are not aware of them at the time, can be drawn out by the teacher issuing a fairly simple challenge. For me this has often taken the form: can you use a single sheet of paper to make a bridge, of span 10cm, capable of supporting a 500g weight?

As soon as the paper and weights are distributed and the supports, which can be books or wooden blocks, decided upon, the children eagerly set to work. Most children immediately begin folding their paper into a zig-zag shape which, of course, adds considerably to the rigidity of the paper in the direction of the folds. It is not long before bridges capable of supporting 200g to 300g are appearing all round the classroom. When the initial excitement and flurry of activity has subsided, attention can be drawn to what it is that makes the paper able to support such loads. Suitable questions are: what is the optimum number of folds? Must all the folds be equally spaced? Does cutting the paper into two or more pieces, to be used in different ways, add to the load it is able to support? Is a tubular shape better than a folded one?

This approach is a far better introduction to rigid structures than discussing strong shapes illustrated in a text-book. The children's interest thus aroused can then be channelled into a study of bridges or building structures.

Bridge structure II

Another challenge which may lead from the paper bridge or be introduced separately is the bridge made from drinking straws. Again, the rules may be modified to suit individual classes and circumstances. The form I have usually issued it in has been: can you use five plastic drinking straws and no more than 5cm of cellophane tape to make the strongest possible bridge of span 10cm? It is amazing how many pieces some children can divide 5cm of tape into! This challenge gives the children scope for experimenting with a great many different designs and I have always allowed them to get ideas by looking at pictures of different bridges.

Incidentally, when it comes to testing the bridge this has been done either by suspending more and more weights until the bridge was about to collapse or by adding sand to a suspended margarine tub bucket until the maximum load was obtained, and weighing the sand.

Other challenges

Other investigations which have been made whose results extended into an exhibition for the rest of the school are making a timing device and making a musical instrument.

In the 'timing device challenge' the children in the fourth year were asked to make and calibrate a device capable of timing, fairly accurately, durations of time up to 2 minutes. Duplicated sheets giving information taken mainly from the *Science 5–13* book *Time*(**1**) were given out and about three weeks, including the half-term holiday, allowed to complete the task.

All of the staff were so impressed by the quality and diversity of the devices produced, that we decided to hold an exhibition to which all the other children in the school were invited. This proved to be a very worthwhile project, since the interest shown by the questions of the younger children and discussion which took place was really most satisfying.

Many children can work apparently carefully and systematically through a series of experiments on musical instruments and yet in the end, be confused about the difference between pitch and loudness. However, if they have actually made simple instruments themselves, they are far more aware of the difference. As part of a piece of work on sound and music, therefore, we have set the children the task of making their own instruments. Suggestions for designs of the different types of instruments and information about how to vary pitch and increase volume, were duplicated and given to the children.

At the end of the project when quite an impressive array of different instruments had been made and displayed, a short concert of suitable music played on the instruments was given by the children.

Conclusions

I hope this chapter has given some insight into one approach to science and provided some suggestions which the reader may try out with his/her class. Teaching is a very personal job and everyone employs slightly different methods. However, it is very important that the children's minds as well as their bodies are active when they are doing science and that is why the tasks and methods suggested here involve not only doing things, but discussing before, during and after the investigations are carried out. It is essential that in our increasingly technological world, our children are brought up to be objective in their assessment of the things that are thrust upon them by advertisers in the name of progress. How many things have been heralded by the advertisers as representing progress when really the main, if not only, merit in them has been cheaper manufacturing costs, which have not necessarily been reflected, at least initially, in the retail price!

If any justification is required for doing the sorts of investigations described above, that of providing real situations in which to employ mathematical skills is surely enough. Sometimes we fool ourselves into thinking that the children in our classes know and can apply many of the skills of measurement because they have worked correctly through some mathematical exercises. However, it is surprising to discover misconceptions in the minds of children when they have to employ some of these skills in real situations. The HMI Primary Survey draws attention to the need to make connections between maths and science in Chapter 5.63(**2**).

When children have a need to develop a new skill in mathematics or any other discipline, their motivation for learning is greatly enhanced. Therefore, in the investigations described here, a conscious decision was made by the teacher, when considering the degree of accuracy required, to tailor each investigation to the ability of the individuals concerned. Sometimes children found themselves employing a skill they had recently learned, while on other occasions a new skill, which they were ready to learn, was needed in order to do the task most effectively.

4

Investigating electric circuits

Pitmaston Junior School caters for approximately 300 children aged 7 to 11 years, and is set in the residential outskirts of Worcester. Science is taught to all classes usually by the class teacher, and may be integrated with other aspects of the curriculum. Some topics are science based while in others the science element is complementary to environmental or geographical aspects. Each class spends the equivalent of 1 to $1\frac{1}{2}$ hours per week on science spread throughout the year.

4

Investigating electric circuits

Colin Heath

Working with simple electrical circuits provides endless fascination and yet many teachers shy away from allowing children to do more than very superficial work on this. There are many reasons for this, not the least being the nagging worry at the back of everyone's mind that electricity can be very dangerous and, therefore, is best left alone. Mains electricity certainly is potentially lethal and under no circumstances should children be allowed to experiment with electrical equipment connected to the mains, even if it is linked through a transformer. Torch batteries, however, do not have the potential to harm any child and, provided it is made clear at the outset that the investigations must only be carried out using low voltage batteries and torch bulbs, there is no danger.

What is electricity?

Electricity is a form of energy obtained by the flow of electrons through a metal or carbon, which then forms a *conductor*. This flow cannot take place through non-metals or compounds, which are, therefore, *insulators*. Electrons can only flow if: a) there is a pushing agent in the system or circuit, e.g., a battery; b) there is no break, or air gap, in the circuit, i.e., the circuit is complete. During their passage through the circuit, electrons are pushed from atom to atom along the wires forming the circuit.

A better idea of the units of electricity may be gained if an analogy is drawn with water in a central heating system. The *voltage* (or *volts*) is the measurement of the pressure of electricity rather like the pressure pushing the water through the pipes. The *current*, measured in *amperes*, or *amps*, is the measure of the flow of electricity, rather like the measure of the amount of water passing through the pipes. Thus water can be at high pressure passing through a very narrow pipe and so the amount of water passing in a given time will not be great. Alternatively, it can be at low pressure passing through a wide pipe, when again the amount of water will be quite small. However, it can be at high pressure and passing through a wide pipe when the amount of water will be vast.

One important difference in this analogy between water and electricity is that if a water pipe is cut or open-ended, water will flow out whereas this is not the case in an electrical circuit. If there is a break or gap in the circuit, electrons will not flow.

Mains electricity has the potential to deliver electrons (electricity) at high pressure and high current sufficient to pass through the body and cause injury. A torch battery, on the other hand, can only deliver electrons at very low pressure and low current flow. This potential is many times less than needed to pass through the body. Such batteries, therefore, can be considered completely safe for children to handle.

The *wattage*, or *watts*, of an electrical appliance is the measure of the power or energy used by it. The relationship between voltage, current (measured in amps), and power used (watts), is, for example:

	Volts	× Amps	= Watts
5 watt night light	250 volts	× 0.02 amps	= 5 watts
	high pressure	× low current	= low power
100 watt bulb	250 volts	× 0.4 amps	= 100 watts
	high pressure	× moderate current	= moderate power
2 kilowatt electric fire	250 volts	× 8 amps	= 2000 watts
	high pressure	× high current	= high power
Car headlamp	12 volts	× 3 amps	= 36 watts
	low pressure	× high current	= moderate power
Torch bulb	2.5 volt	× 0.3 amps	= 0.78 watts
	low pressure	× low current	= low power

Apparatus

One of the features of modern technology is the sealed, never to be repaired, throw away and replace unit. These are found in radio and television sets, washing machines, cars, and even torches. Rarely can a child watch a TV repair man get out a soldering iron, remove a burnt out component and replace it with a new one. Today, a new module is plugged in by the repair man, the set is taken to the workshop for an expert to fix, or else it is pronounced beyond repair! It is very exasperating for inquisitive children to be confronted by these sealed units of 'magic', and therefore they should be given the bare bones or basic items for their early work in electricity. For example, a bulb holder may be a very convenient method of holding a torch bulb and making connections to it, but it is better to allow children to discover for themselves by experimentation which parts of the bulb are the terminals. When a child has done this, he or she will understand how the contacts are made with the bulbholder and will not attribute to it any magic or mystery. This early but very important stage is completely missed out if some 'science kits' are purchased for class use.

50 *Starting primary science*

What are the basic items for early work in electricity for children in the 7 to 9 year age group?

i) *Torch bulbs* These are available rated at 2.5 volts, 3.5 volts and 6 volts. It is probably better to use only the 2.5 volt bulbs initially and to have a few 3.5 volt and 6 volt bulbs available for extension work. A collection of sound and 'burnt out' mains bulbs (clear not pearl), car headlamp bulbs and perhaps projector lamps are useful for the children to examine.

ii) *Batteries* A selection of the types most commonly used in torches should be available, e.g. SP2, SP11, No. 6 and No. 800 (cycle lamp battery). These are either single cell or twin cell batteries. Note—if the flat $4\frac{1}{2}$ volt battery (No. 1289) is provided, then a 3.5 volt bulb must be used with it. For most of the work the 3 volt cycle lamp battery is probably the most versatile and economical.

iii) *Wires* The greater the variety of types, sizes and thicknesses provided for the children, the more interesting their investigations will be. For later work a single stranded, plastic covered copper wire is easiest for the children to handle. This is obtainable either from educational suppliers or locally, as single core low voltage bell flex.

iv) *Crocodile clips* These are very useful for making connections and a set of wires about 30cm long with crocodile clips attached to the ends is very handy.

v) *Bulb holders* (miniature Edison screw type) These, for torch bulbs, are useful for such work as lighting more than one bulb at a time.

vi) A collection of common objects made of metals and non-metals is needed for work on conductors and insulators.

vii) *Optional extras* A low voltage electric bell and/or buzzer, bell push, switches (various types) and low voltage D.C. motor are all useful for extension work.

Activities

Making a simple circuit

The first investigation with electricity for young children should be to light a torch bulb from a battery. For this provide a 2.5 volt bulb, a single cell battery (e.g. SP11), a collection of wires of various types and thicknesses (some bare and some covered), and metal objects like wire paper clips, scissors, nails, kitchen foil, etc.

Questions for the children to consider and investigate are:

a) Can you light the bulb using different wires?

b) Does the colour of the plastic coating on the wiring make any difference to the brightness of the bulb?
c) Is thick wire better than thin wire?
d) Is wire covered with a plastic, rubber or cotton coating better than that without?
e) Why are most wires used to carry electricity covered with either plastic or rubber?
f) Can the electricity from the battery jump a very, very small gap?

Most children soon discover a way of lighting the bulb. For those who have difficulty, a few clues like pointing out places where wires may be connected soon get them working again. Suitable questions to ask about the bulb are:

g) Which part lights up?
h) What do you think this part is made from?
i) What do you think it makes light up?
j) Can you trace the path of the electricity through the bulb?
k) If you reverse the position of the wires leading from the battery, does the bulb still light up?
l) A logical but rarely asked question is: if you put two sets of wires from the battery to the bulb, does it make the bulb twice as bright?

Children who have considered all these questions will have had a much better introduction to electricity and simple circuits than those who have connected terminal 1 to terminal 2 and terminal 3 to terminal 4, etc.

For those who do not know the answers to these questions the following information will be helpful, although there is no substitute for trying for oneself.

a) The wire used for electrical work is usually made from copper and may be single or multistranded. Copper is the best conductor of electricity among the common metals. If soft iron wire is among the samples used to complete the circuit, it may give a duller light than copper because it is not such a good conductor.

b) Before the wires are joined or connected, about 2cm of the plastic or rubber coating must be removed to expose the copper wire. Electricity cannot flow through the covering, which is an insulator. The colour of the covering is merely for ease of identification.

c) The energy required to light a torch bulb is very small, and therefore there will probably be no difference between the brightness of the bulb whether thin or thick wire is used. An electrical appliance which uses a great deal of electric current, e.g. an electric kettle or fire, requires quite thick wire in order to avoid the wire being overloaded and becoming hot.

52 *Starting primary science*

d, e) Electric wire is insulated to prevent short circuits, that is, to prevent the electrons taking a short cut and rushing back to the battery without going through the bulb.

f) In subdued light, it is just possible to see a tiny spark jump the minute gap between the wires when completing the circuit.

g) Inside the bulb can be seen the filament (the part which lights up).

h, i) It is made from the metal tungsten through which electrons (electricity) cannot move easily. Because they are pushed along it by the battery, the wire first becomes hot, then red hot and finally white hot giving out white light. This happens very quickly. When a battery is nearly drained of current, the bulb filament can be seen merely to glow orange rather like an electric fire element, which is made of the same metal but much thicker. If the wire in the bulb is too thin for the amount of electricity going through it, it melts. This is why a 2.5 volt bulb should only be used with up to a 3 volt battery and a 3.5 volt bulb with up to a 4.5 volt battery.

j) The path of the electrons (electricity) through the bulb is shown in the following diagram.

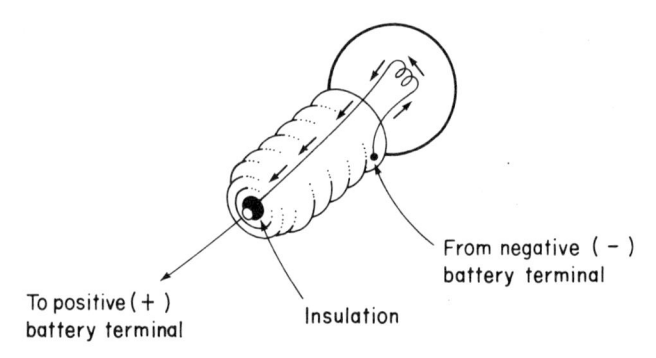

Figure 9

k) Although in a torch the screw on the bulb is usually connected to the negative, that is the zinc outer case of the battery, it does not matter which way round it is connected.

One difference between the current supplied by a torch battery and the mains supply is that while the battery has a positive (+) and negative (−) terminal and electrons flow constantly in one direction only, i.e. direct current (DC), the terminals in the mains system alternate from positive to negative 50 times per second (50 cycles), that is, in alternating current (AC). An electric motor as fitted to model train sets and racing cars does reverse its direction of rotation when the flow of electrons is reversed.

1) The question whether two sets of wires make the bulb twice as bright is an interesting one. The electrical energy supplied by the battery is used mainly by the electrons struggling through the filament of the bulb. Providing that one pair of wires is capable of carrying the necessary current, the addition of an extra pair of wires will have no effect. If thin wires are used to carry electricity to something which consumes a large amount of energy, e.g. an electric kettle or heater, then they will become overloaded, get hot and maybe melt. This is the purpose of the fuse in a domestic system. The fuse is made from a wire which melts easily and so, if the system is overloaded and the wiring gets hot, the fuse wire will melt and break the circuit before damage is done to the main wiring and insulation.

Conductors and insulators

When children have examined a torch bulb and made a circuit to light it using a battery and various conductors, the next series of investigations should be into conductors and non-conductors (or insulators). I have found the following system most convenient to use in the classroom.

A collection of various small objects should be provided for the children to place between the two drawing pin terminals to see if they conduct

3·5 volt bulb in bulbholder

Wood block approx. 15cm x 7cm x 1cm

4·5 volt battery

Drawing pin terminals

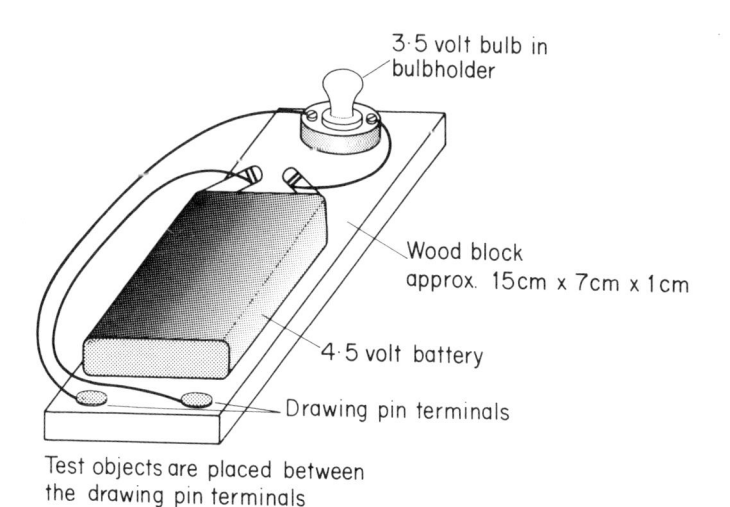

Test objects are placed between the drawing pin terminals

Figure 10

electricity and complete the circuit. Interesting items include: coins (both cupro nickel and cupro bronze), nails, screws (brass and steel), samples of various woods, various types of plastic, glass (e.g. small bottle), metallized foil, aluminium foil, a piece of coke, charcoal, pencil lead (various grades from H to 3B), fine chain (e.g. necklace), carbon rod from battery, hair clips and grips, etc.

Items like coke and pencil lead are interesting because they are partial conductors of electricity. If a good contact is made with them, the bulb will light up but be dimmer than when metal is used.

With pencil lead, graphite, the hardness is achieved by adding clay, therefore a soft pencil will conduct electricity better than a hard one. Graphite (carbon) is used in this way to make dimming devices and volume controls for transistor radios. The carbon rod from a battery is made from almost pure carbon, tightly packed, and conducts electricity equally as well as copper wire. Chain made from silver or alloys may provide an interesting discussion point. When it is stretched fairly tightly a good contact is made between the links and electricity is conducted, but when it is laid loosely across the terminals on the test board, there are spaces between the links and electricity is not conducted. Hair pins and grips are often coated with shellac or plastic, therefore although made from metal, they do not conduct unless the coating has been damaged, exposing the bare metal at the points where contact is made.

When all the available samples have been tested and sorted into those which do and do not conduct electricity, the children should be able to make generalizations about what conductors are made from.

An interesting extension is to attach two wires to the terminals of the circuit board and immerse the ends in liquids. Although pure water is a non-conductor the addition of common salt or vinegar will turn it into a partial conductor. Moving the two wires closer together increases the brightness of the light from the bulb. Bubbles are observed to appear on the wires in the water. It is probably better merely to note their existence and not try to go into explanations of electrolysis of water. A useful safety point can be made, though, that water can be a conductor and therefore electric appliances, plugs or switches should never be handled with wet hands.

Using more than one single celled battery

A battery is really a battery of cells. The torch battery with which we are all familiar is either single celled, giving a little over 1.5 volts when new, or a number of cells linked together. Such batteries, therefore, are available giving multiples of 1.5 volts, i.e. 3 volts, 4.5 volts, 6 volts, 9 volts, etc. Most torches work on 3 volts, 4.5 volts or 6 volts.

A very useful investigation for children is to join two single cells in various ways and connect them to a 2.5 volt bulb. The arrangements shown below may be suggested and the children asked which arrangement gives:

a) a dull light
b) a bright light
c) no light

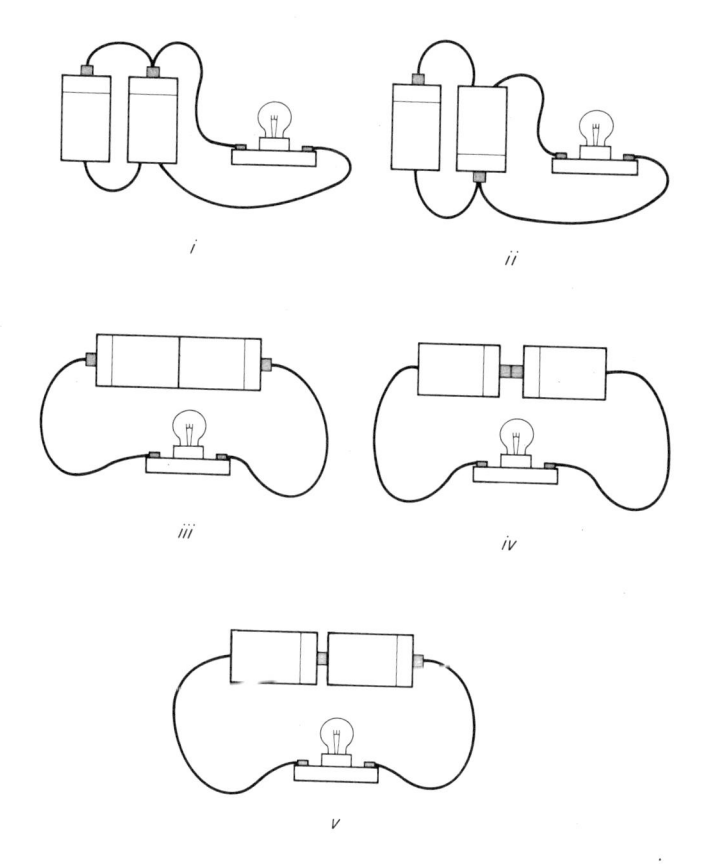

i

ii

iii

iv

v

Figure 11

Notice that a bulb holder is used for convenience in these experiments.

In arrangement *i)* the batteries are pushing in the same direction but the amount of 'push' is the same as obtained from one battery, i.e. 1.5 volts. However, the push can be sustained for twice as long. The batteries are said to be acting in parallel. A dull light is obtained.

Arrangement *ii)* theoretically should not produce enough pushing power to light the bulb, because the batteries are working against each other. If one battery has significantly more power than the other, the difference will pass on to the bulb and cause it to glow.

The third arrangement *iii*) has the two positive sides of the cells connected to the bulb and therefore, there is no complete circuit for the electrons and no light from the bulb.

Arrangement *iv*) is similar to the third arrangement. The two negative sides of the cells are connected to the bulb and consequently there is no complete circuit made.

In arrangement *v*) the two cells are working together and adding to each other so there is double the pushing power (3 volts) and double the brightness of the bulb. The cells are said to be arranged in series, i.e., one after the other.

An extension to this series of experiments is to provide a 3.5 volt bulb and three single cell batteries. (A 3.5 volt bulb is required because a series arrangement of the three cells will give 4.5 volts which, if it does not burn out the 2.5 volt bulb immediately, will certainly shorten its useful life.)

The task set for the children is to link the three cells in various ways and say which arrangement gives:

    a) no light
    b) a very dull light
    c) a dull light
    d) a bright light

It is very difficult for one child to hold and make connections to three single cell batteries, but two children working together can just manage it.

If it is intended to proceed from the two cell arrangements to three cell arrangements, it is probably better to begin with a 3.5 volt bulb and use it for all the experiments, thereby giving a better impression of the varying pushing power or voltage from the different arrangements. Fairly new batteries are then essential.

Lighting more than one bulb from a battery

Following from the previous set of experiments with single celled batteries, the next investigation could be lighting more than one bulb at the same time. This utilizes the concepts of series and parallel wiring introduced in that section.

Before allowing children to begin any investigation where they are asked to arrange circuits, it is essential to mention the *short circuit*. Batteries are relatively expensive items and if short circuited will be almost drained of useful energy in less than half an hour. I explain to the children (who have worked through the earlier activity of lighting a torch bulb by connecting wires to it from a battery), that electricity, like people, is lazy.

If the electricity (electrons) is able to rush from one side (terminal) of the battery to the other without doing any work, it will do so. When all the electricity has rushed 'home', there will be none left to use in lighting the bulb, or anything else. Therefore we *never*, ever, connect a wire straight from one terminal of the battery to the other. Children can see the logic in this argument and will check their circuits while working to ensure they are not offering a 'short cut' for the electricity. They have to work, so why shouldn't the electricity!

Although these experiments can be carried out using two 2.5 volt bulbs (in bulbholders) and a single cell battery, it is preferable to provide a 3 volt battery, e.g. a cycle lamp battery No. 800.

Initially the children tend to try a number of arrangements for connecting two bulbs to the battery and soon there is quite a tangle of wires. After a short period of experimentation, the children should be encouraged to work tidily and keep the connecting wires fairly straight and orderly. If this is not done they will find it very difficult to draw diagrams of their arrangements.

The two systems of connecting the bulbs are series and parallel wiring, although there are some variations on them.

The *parallel* system is the one used for all domestic wiring where each appliance can draw the full voltage available. The children's arrangements will basically be as follows:

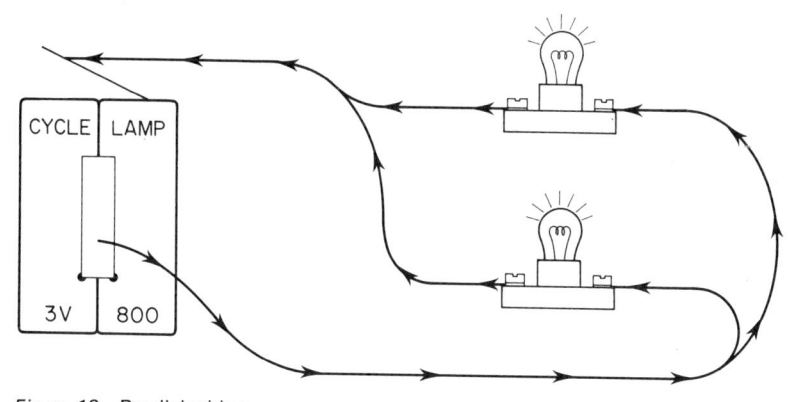

Figure 12 Parallel wiring

Each bulb can draw electrons which can return straight to the battery without passing through the other bulb. In effect both bulbs are independent of each other.

On tracing the path of the electrons travelling round the *series* arrangement you will notice that they have to struggle through first one and then the other bulb before returning to the battery. In this system, if one bulb is removed (or is broken), the circuit is not complete and neither bulb

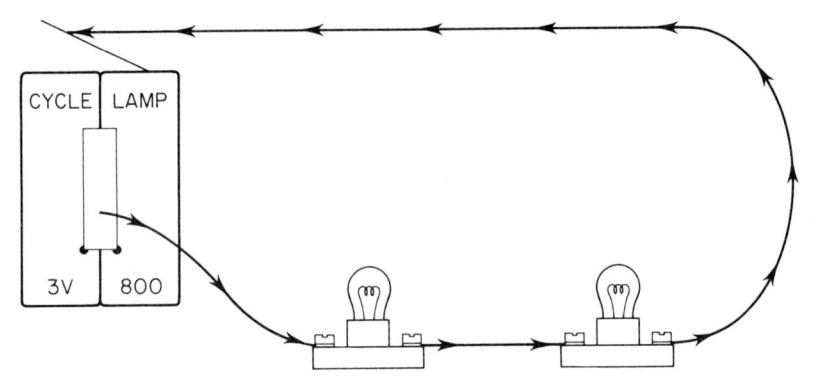

Figure 13 Series wiring

will light up. When both bulbs are connected they are sharing the electrical energy and are only about half as bright as they would be if they had all the energy. The most common example of this arrangement is the Christmas tree lights where 240 volts is shared between 20 bulbs drawing 12 volts or 40 bulbs of 6 volts each.

If a third bulb is added the number of combinations increases. All three can be wired in parallel or series fashion or there can be a mixture of each.

Switches

From the work already described, the children should learn that a switch contains no 'magic' and is merely a convenient way of breaking and making a circuit. There are disadvantages to the miniature switch (similar to the domestic light switch) for most work, since the children

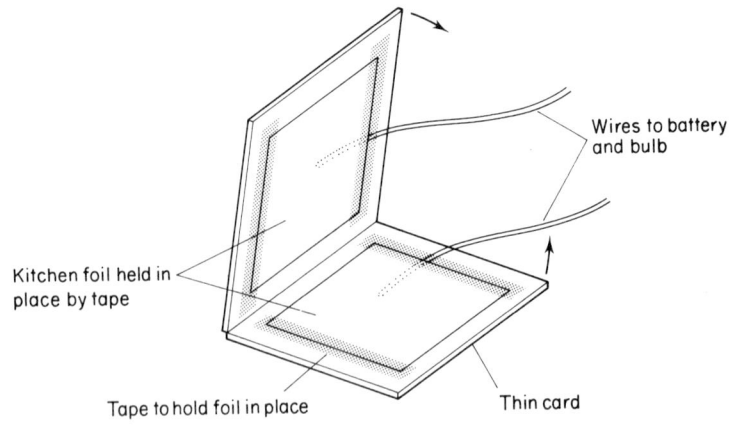

Figure 14

Investigating electric circuits 59

are inclined to leave the system switched on for long periods, thereby draining the battery unnecessarily. A far better arrangement is a home made press switch. One which children can easily make is shown in Figure 14 opposite. It is quick and simple to make and yet is very effective.

When making this switch, care should be taken to ensure the plastic from the ends of the wire is first removed in order that contact is made with the kitchen foil.

Another simple switch which can be made or assembled by the children uses a paper clip, drawing pins and either a piece of soft wood or soft hardboard of the type used for classroom display boards, as seen in Figure 15 below.

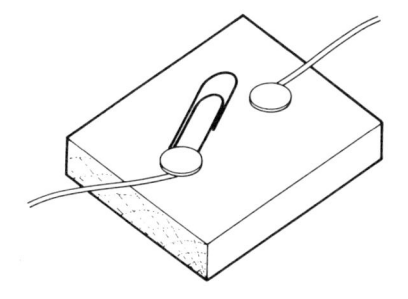

Figure 15

The third type of switch which can be made fairly easily uses a piece of tin plate cut from a food tin. Care must be taken to ensure that all sharp edges are removed by using either a fine file or emery paper. A safer variation can be made by using a strip of flexible plastic (e.g. from the lid of a soft margarine or cottage cheese tub), completely covered with kitchen foil, as in Figure 16. A number of these switches can be made and kept ready for use.

Some children enjoy making their own switch arrangements for model traffic lights and this can be done quite easily using the paper clip type switch, as in Figure 17 overleaf.

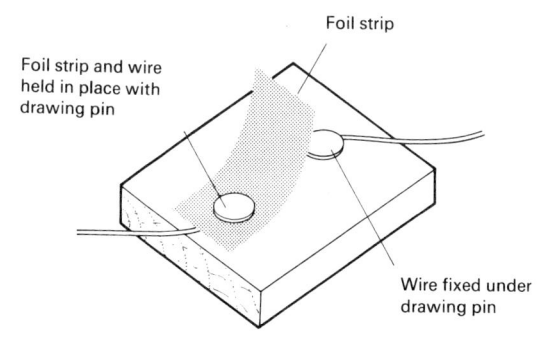

Foil strip

Foil strip and wire held in place with drawing pin

Wire fixed under drawing pin

Figure 16

60 *Starting primary science*

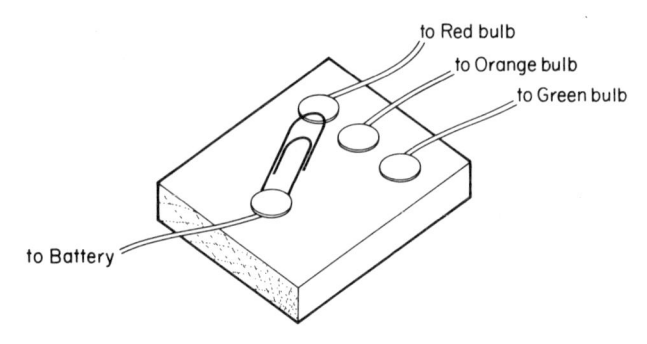

Figure 17

For those children who are familiar with bulbs and batteries the arrangement for two-way switches of the type used to turn on a light from either of two switches is fascinating. Again, the paper clip type switch is the best system to use. In a two-way switch, contact is always made with one or the other of the two terminals. The switch positions are shown below.

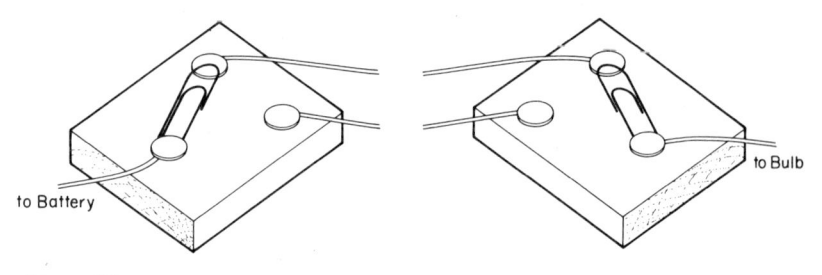

Figure 18

Further activities

Children who have been helped and encouraged to carry out the activities described in this section will have an understanding of the basic principles of electric circuits. Their further investigations may be enhanced by the availability of an electric bell or buzzer and a small electric motor. With these additional items there are endless extension activities which, either as individuals or groups, they may engage in. For example, they can make working model robots, lighthouses, burglar alarms, Morse code transmitters and receivers as well as wiring lights in play houses.

Conclusions

If all children are given the opportunity to investigate simple electric circuits in the way described, they will grow up into adults who can appreciate something of the circuitry in domestic appliances, and, while having a respect for electricity, will not have an irrational fear of it.

The activities described here are well within the capabilities of young children from the age of 6 or 7 upwards. There are many extensions to this work, including electromagnetism which may be developed from the age of 9 years.

5
Small mammals in the classroom

Abbey Park First School is located in Pershore, a small town within the rural setting of the Vale of Evesham.

The school has approximately 200 boys and girls on roll with ages ranging from 5 to 9 years, and a teaching establishment of head + 7. There is no formal timetable for science, the subject forming part of project/topic work in the lower part of the school and environmental studies with the older children occupying about 50% of their weekly programme. All staff teach science in some form each term, and one member of staff acts as school adviser for the subject.

5
Small mammals in the classroom
Alex Wall

Animals can be enormously useful in the primary classroom. Most children love animals and small mammals can be of great value not just for teaching science, but for aiding the moral and social development of young children. If a teacher wants to introduce animals into the classroom, there are many sources of information and help available. But, whether one wants to keep one animal or several, the first matter to be decided is, which animal(s)? The R.S.P.C.A. in their practical and helpful booklet *Animals in Schools* (**1**), recommend six species:

> rat (hooded or albino)
> mouse
> gerbil
> rabbit
> hamster
> guinea pig

It is highly advisable to check on your county's Health and Safety at Work policy regarding the keeping of animals before an acquisition is made, although there should be no objection to any of the animals listed.

The final choice will obviously depend upon availability. Pet shops, high schools, colleges, or university zoology departments are all potentially good sources.

In our school we have never kept hamsters or guinea pigs and, therefore, are not competent to discuss the merits or otherwise of these animals. We have, however, successfully kept all the other species listed above and our first choice would always be the hooded rat. Rats, unfortunately, suffer from bad public relations, but they are clean, lively, friendly, intelligent animals. Of all those listed, when treated correctly, they are least likely to bite (no child has yet been bitten by a rat in our school), they are certainly the cleanest and—an important quality when working with young children—because of their relatively slow movements and large size they are quite easily handled. Their natural inquisitiveness is also a point in their favour when carrying out experimental, behavioural work in the classroom.

Mice, also, are friendly, inquisitive animals and provide an interesting comparison with the rats and it would be a shame to exclude them.

However, their only disadvantage is that the male has a distinctive odour! It is not lack of cleanliness but a device for defining territory and if male mice are kept they really need to be cleaned out daily because the smell can be offensive. The female mouse does not smell at all and on her own is an admirable choice if breeding is not part of the programme.

The gerbil also provides for comparison between species and has one outstanding characteristic. Originally it was a desert animal and lived in burrows. If kept in a glass tank filled with silver sand or sawdust woodshavings with straw, the animals will create fascinating burrows which change daily as they make new excavations. Gerbils do, however, have a tendency to nip occasionally, and if two are kept together they may, after sharing a cage quite happily for two or three years, suddenly begin to fight, often to the death. This is not inevitable, but is a distinct possibility with which one must reckon.

It would be a pity for any first school to be without rabbits, yet in terms of overall interest, they would be fourth in our list of priorities. Perhaps the prime reason for keeping rabbits is to breed, because there are few sights more pleasurable for young children than that of a baby rabbit. However, baby rabbits grow into big rabbits and they may become quite vicious. Also, for very young children, they may be too big to handle easily, although for children of seven and over, they are quite manageable. In terms of narrow educational work the scope the rabbit offers is limited, but the final decision depends on the reason for keeping the animals in the first place.

Care and management of animals

In general, rules concerning the welfare of animals require only common sense, but it is worth remembering that there is a legal obligation to ensure that no animal is caused unnecessary suffering. Thus, cages must be of the correct size (for all information relating to cages etc. see the R.S.P.C.A. booklet), the animal must always have fresh food and clean water and must be kept in a clean condition.

The venture can be quite expensive, but there are ways to lower costs. Cages will certainly be the most expensive items. They may be purchased from pet shops or educational suppliers, but do consider first looking around your own school; are there any old aquaria which could be adapted to a new purpose? Our cages were mostly obtained from a neighbouring school which no longer kept animals. In fact, thanks to gifts, loans and adapting old cages, not a single cage has been bought.

Bedding, usually sawdust, can also be expensive, but is there a wood merchant nearby who will provide it free of charge? All of our sawdust comes from the local undertaker!

Straw for nesting material can be bought, but again, if you are in a rural area, a local farmer will surely be able to provide the odd bale now and then.

Water bottles and food now remain the only two items to account for. Obviously the food bill increases with the number of animals kept and whether it is met from capitation allowance, school fund or monies raised by the P.T.A., is a matter for each individual school.

Care of animals during the weekends and holidays may present a problem and this is something which should be resolved before a decision to keep animals is made. There are three choices. Either the teacher assumes responsibility all of the time, or the children assume that responsibility, or it is shared. Shared responsibility would seem to be the best solution as it allows the teacher to have a break. In our school, the children usually look after the animals during the long summer holidays and occasionally at other holiday times, while the teacher cares for them at weekends and half-terms and so on.

Although all of the animals suggested by the R.S.P.C.A. are domestic, unless they are treated carefully and correctly, they will soon become less than tame, at which point it would be unsafe to allow children to handle them. From a beginner's point of view, therefore, it is wise to acquire the animals as young as possible, preferably soon after weaning, in order that a programme of handling and taming may begin. To guarantee tameness, the animals must be used to handling, which means on a daily basis. Advice on this can be found in most handbooks. With all species but the rabbit, it is best to place both hands slowly and gently around the animal and to scoop it up. The rabbit is picked up by the scruff of the neck, supported beneath its hind quarters with the other hand. It is also important to remember that young animals can be over-handled.

Introducing the animals into the classroom

Children and teachers obviously need confidence when dealing with animals, and confidence breeds confidence just as fear breeds fear, so it is advisable to introduce the animals to the classroom one at a time. The children need to be prepared for this new event, as it would surely be unfair to them and to the animals suddenly to swamp the classroom with a host of different livestock. Once the children have learned to care for and respect one animal, then new and perhaps even stranger ones may be brought into the classroom.

In our school, we began with rats and went on to rabbits, gerbils, ducks and bees. The animal we next wished to introduce was the mouse and after some initial difficulty in finding some domestic mice, we were promised one male and one female that were just weaned. Disposing of unwanted mice seems to be a universal problem and instead of the expected two, there came a batch of twelve, at all stages of development in one box! Unfortunately, the twelve multiplied before we could separate them and after the first problem of sorting male from female, we were faced with the task of taming the adult mice which in fact were quite wild. By this time the children were very used to dealing with animals in all sorts of strange situations and despite my insistence that initially they wore rubber gloves to protect themselves from bites, two young girls refused to do so and handled them with bare hands yet suffered no bites. If those mice had been in that classroom twelve months previously, no one would have dared go near them. Thus, familiarization with animals can breed confidence in children, a confidence which has tremendous influence on all aspects of the child's personality and school work.

However, even the most confident and competent person at some time may suffer a scratch or a bite and if this is dealt with sensibly, it need cause no real upset. Apart from cleaning the wound and applying antiseptic cream, it is important to check either with the school records or with the child's parent that the child has undergone a course of anti-tetanus injections. Certainly from time to time a child will be bitten or scratched, but this is very rare and in no way detracts from the fun and interest of keeping animals in the classroom.

A programme of experiments to study animal behaviour

One reason for keeping animals in the classroom is that they provide for the children a permanent centre of interest throughout the year. It is a reason to look forward to coming to school, especially, for example, when the doe rabbit is expecting young, and it provides an immediate stimulus for discussion and work across all areas of the curriculum. How the individual teacher exploits that stimulus will depend upon the conditions in the class and the school, but once the animals have been acquired it is important to be aware of the possibilities for study which they offer.

The following suggestions are an amalgam of experiments carried out by children in the seven to nine age range. There is no definite order to these experiments and within each there is the possibility for an almost infinite number of variables. The only determining factors are time and organization.

The experiments are the results of three years' work with different children and different animals. At the end of a given period a great deal of statistical information on the animals' behavioural activity was accumulated. The fact that the children knew that a particular rat had a preference for square shapes which were coloured red and that she went more frequently through a hole of that shape if presented with peanuts, preferably dry roasted, on the other side, was neither here nor there. It provided the children with material to think and to talk about, whatever their intellectual level. The introduction to this book explains in detail the ethos behind science in the First school. What is necessary here is a reminder that throughout this programme it is not the results that matter but the approach through observation, hypothesis, experimentation, recording results, and synthesis.

One reason—perhaps the most interesting one—for using animals in this context is that there is no such thing as a wrong result. If the child is observing carefully, what he or she actually sees is the result. Although all of the suggested experiments presuppose certain behavioural traits in healthy, happy animals, the interest in using animals, for the child as well as the teacher, is that they are not automatons programmed to respond to certain stimuli and there is, therefore, no guaranteed outcome. Each new experiment is an entirely original experience.

Although any of these experiments could be taken in isolation, they tend to follow a logical pattern. That pattern can obviously only be determined by the behaviour of the animal and if the animal behaves in a way which opens new possibilities for study, then the planned experiments must be abandoned and a new line of approach followed. This suggested dynamism should become clearer in the description of the programme of experiments.

Observation of behaviour

All that is needed for this very simple experiment is an animal and a clean surface. Beyond that, it is entirely up to the teacher how he or she wishes the lesson to proceed. All the experimental work described here can be carried out either as a class activity or in small groups, but if the maximum benefit is to be gained, small group work is ideal. More than one animal in the classroom enables several small groups to be engaged in a similar activity at the same time, which makes the teacher's organization much easier. Whether or not the children are to be provided with a pencil and paper initially is for the teacher to decide, but perhaps for the first time, discussion and observation is enough, enabling the children to become aware of certain features and to share those observations. The role of the teacher in encouraging the children to make relevant observations is vital.

This period of observation may be extended or curtailed according to circumstances, but if it is the children's first experience of such animals, then to allow them to observe each one in detail is a useful and valid exercise.

The type and degree of observation will vary according to age and intellectual level, but it might be composed of an initial period of simple observation with discussion, followed by a period spent drawing or painting the animal and then a third period during which a written description of the animal is produced.

The teacher can encourage the children to make accurate, close observations with hints and questions. Often, however, the most astute observations come from the children. It is they who point out that rats, mice and gerbils appear to have a different number of toes on the hind and fore feet. It is they who will notice that one gerbil has a slightly crooked tail and the other has a straight tail. They will notice the colour of the eyes but it might be the teacher who has to ask them the colour of the claws of the gerbil, and so on. Children of any age, at any intellectual level, can take part in this simple physical description.

Breeding

The visual observation can be followed by finding its weight. Besides giving a little more information about a specific animal, this enables comparisons to be made between, say, male and female. Soon, generalizations can be made when the children realize that the male is generally heavier than the female.

This physical description can be very excitingly extended when it comes to breeding. Here, the rabbits come into their own! Conception is almost guaranteed and it is much easier to convince reluctant parents that their son or daughter really does want a baby rabbit to take home rather than a baby rat! Perhaps it is an obvious point, but when breeding from school animals, it is essential to ensure that there is a way of accommodating the young after the school no longer has a need for them.

Through breeding animals, the child very naturally becomes aware of birth and birth control. If we want the rabbits to be born during school time, we need to know the length of oestrus cycle when the buck and doe are left together, we need to know for how long the doe will be pregnant. After the birth we need to know how much time can safely elapse before we can handle the baby rabbits, and when the young are finally weaned, when it is safe to breed again and at what age to stop breeding. This, of course, is common to all species, and the relevant information may be found in the R.S.P.C.A. booklet. For a rabbit, however, there is not true oestrus cycle, gestation is between 28–31 days and it is safe to handle after ten days. The young are fully weaned at 49 days.

Again one can chart, after 10 days, the daily growth until the young are weaned and observe the natural differences between the strongest and weakest in the litter.

Behavioural characteristics

With smaller mammals, in addition to the physical description, there is also the description of the activities of the animal during the period of observation. This is most important because it is the foundation for all future work. Using the rat, mouse and gerbil, it soon becomes apparent that they share certain behavioural characteristics. Perhaps the first thing that comes to mind is movement. How does the animal move? How can its movements be described? Do all of the animals move in the same way? Is their movement random or is there a purpose to it? A child might suggest that this is a totally new experience for the animals, it might be exploring. This, indeed, is probably true. One of the next tasks is to try to find out if the animal is exploring; is it exploring at random, or is there a method, and can it remember what it has explored? The possibilities here are almost infinite but some possible future experiments will be listed in the next section.

Again, a child might notice that all three species appear to stand on their hind legs for quite a lot of the time. When do they do this? Why do they do it? This activity is known as rearing, but it presents another behavioural feature to be studied.

It is quite apparent that all of the animals spend a great deal of time sniffing. Why do they do this? Is their sense of smell better than ours? Which other senses do they use? Creating simple experiments to test this may be difficult, but the children can at least be made aware of it and simple visual discrimination experiments will be listed under shape and colour preference beginning on p. 74.

If a handful of food is scattered on the surface, it is interesting to note first what the food consists of, and whether or not the animal seems to prefer one particular food. A simple food choice experiment can be set up to study this more methodically. All of our animals have shown a distinct preference for sunflower seeds, and it is fascinating just to watch how the animal eats the seed. There does seem to be a method in the position in which it holds the seed to crack the outer shell and then remove the kernel. Through close and detailed observation the children can be made aware of this.

During the first period of observation, it will become apparent that the animals tend to spend a long time grooming. Is there a pattern to this grooming? Do they clean behind their ears before they clean their faces or do they clean their body before the head? A pattern does emerge within the species and between species.

Lastly, the animal may be totally unco-operative and either do nothing or sleep! This, however, is a valid observation because most small rodents are not diurnal but are active mostly at dawn and dusk. Unfortunately, it would seem that there is not enough time in the school day to study this in depth, but perhaps a record might be kept of the activity or lack of it at hourly intervals during the day.

Exploring behaviour

Having decided that the animal appears to be exploring, the problem now is how to set up an experiment whereby this can be measured. The children think that the animal is exploring; they now need to test that hypothesis. A situation must be created where exploratory behaviour is the factor which is being studied and recorded. The children, therefore, need some understanding of the concept of control of scientific experiments. This is a rather difficult concept to teach to young children and one possible method of conveying some understanding of it is through exaggeration. A very unsubtle example which the children could grasp would be to test their ability to hear a pin drop and to play Beethoven's 9th Symphony at the same time! They would soon suggest that it was an unfair test and this is all that could be asked of them. Therefore, to make a fair test of the rodent's exploratory behaviour we need to look at the requirements of the experiment. We need an animal and something to explore. The first thing that comes to mind is a cage.

Exploring an empty cage
It is interesting to allow the children to suggest alternatives and very soon they will realize that the cage to be explored must be empty. We have always used a spare glass aquarium. Glass sides are obviously suitable for viewing and the size is convenient because it measures 30cm × 60cm. This can then be plotted, either by the child or the teacher onto squared paper, to give a plan view of the cage. Depending on the age and ability of the child, games can be played by putting an object into the cage and asking the child to put a finger in the corresponding place on the plan. When the child is competent at this, it is the turn of the animal to be placed in the cage. The child, without taking pencil from paper, follows the animal wherever it goes in the cage. The length of time that the animal remains in the cage is relevant and five minutes would seem to be a reasonable suggestion, although obviously this can be varied. Once again, in terms of control, the question arises—if one animal is in the cage for five minutes, and another for ten minutes, can the results be interpreted meaningfully, or has the experiment in some way changed?

The first time that one group of nine year old girls carried out this experiment they were very upset because of the apparent scribble that appeared on their pages, and on a subsequent attempt they didn't allow any lines to cross so that it appeared much neater. Obviously, the 'scribble' was the meaningful result. The greater the number of animals, the greater the possibility for comparison of results, although if the school only possesses one animal, the experiment may be repeated either immediately or at intervals of days or weeks, and a pattern soon emerges. All rodents tend to remain close to the edge, be it open or walled. This behavioural trait is known as wall-seeking or edge-keeping. As a teacher, one is aware of this instinct but for the children it is a new experience and even for the teacher, each time brings new insights.

A bright child might suggest that the cage used, although constant and, therefore, controlled, was relatively larger for the mice and gerbils than for the rats and this can lead to experiments with larger cages, although it might be difficult to match the ratio of size of animal to size of cage.

Once this pattern of wall-seeking is established, the question arises of why the animal so rarely crosses the cage. One reason which the children might suggest is fear and this is probably the main one, and so the next stage inevitably suggests itself. Can we, in any way, induce the animal to overcome its fear?

The possibilities within this experiment are endless. Similar experiments have been carried out by various groups of children, but their main interest was to try to create an environment where a rodent would cross the centre of a control cage. Some children suggested putting objects in the centre of the cage and recording the number of times the animals approached them. This simple experiment offers many potential lines of study, including varying the object itself. Some children used stones collected from the garden, others used wooden maths cubes. The cubes offer greater potential giving rise to such questions as, why cubes? Wouldn't other solids be equally valid or might the rodent have a preference for a particular solid? The colour of the solids also offers possible lines of study. The only limit is time. The children did not have the time to pursue those ideas further, but the seeds of questioning were sown as they began to realize the complexities of the problem. However, they were able to study the importance of the quantity of cubes and as they had expected, as the number of cubes in the cage was increased, so the number of approaches made by the animal increased, until it could quite confidently cross the centre of the cage.

Learning behaviour

This experiment follows on quite naturally from the last. Now that it has been established that the animals appear to behave methodically and in set patterns when presented with new learning experiences, it is a natural progression for the children to wonder whether an animal can remember what it has learned. This also provides useful discussion on learning and reward because the children will readily see that if there is no apparent purpose to learning (after all, why should a rat want to learn?) then learning will not take place! If anyone doubts this, then a control experiment with no reward can be run consecutively and results compared. What now has to be decided is what task the animals should be encouraged to perform and learn and what reward they should be offered.

Using a maze
A very simple yet interesting possibility is a maze. The construction of the maze can vary in complexity and the number of possible wrong turns can be increased or decreased and results compared. Time taken to complete the maze is also a factor which can be easily measured and taken into account.

At times, children have constructed cardboard mazes to rival that at Hampton Court, but nothing so intricate is required to achieve interesting results. Some of the most rewarding experiments have been carried out in a maze made only of large building blocks. The children are capable of designing mazes which are highly complex, but if a limit on the number of possible wrong turns is imposed, then to design and build one is a task most children in the first school will relish.

The number of possible wrong turns is an entirely personal choice, but since time is often limited, five would be adequate. This, of course, does not mean that the animal can only make a maximum of five mistakes, because each time an error is made, it is counted, even when the animal continually makes that error.

The reward at the end of the maze can be left for the children to choose with the teacher's help. They will probably know what the animal likes best. Tastes differ, but chocolate is often a favourite, closely followed by peanuts and sunflower seeds.

In some early experiments using rats, it was agreed after long discussion to withold their food for twenty-four hours before the experiment. In retrospect, this decision was probably morally wrong. One child suggested that if the rat was to be starved for twenty-four hours we should also eat nothing. The decision was also probably breaking the law relating to cruelty to animals. Future experiments using animals fed on their normal diet but offered tit-bits as reward produced equally interesting results and did not pose any moral dilemma.

Comparing results
Various possibilities exist to compare results using different rewards and this might overlap to some extent with food choice experiments. One possible method is to mark the correct path through the maze by laying a trail using food, and as the animal follows the trail to remove one piece on each attempt until it has learnt the maze. For a first attempt this is a difficult task to measure and control and so it is probably easier to have the reward only in a container at the end of the maze.

The next step is to decide on the number of times the animal should be allowed to go through the maze. A convenient number of times to permit the animal to attempt the maze would seem to be ten. This number could be reduced although the fewer the number of times, the less likely learning is to take place. From various sets of results collated by different groups of children, it does seem that the animals begin to show positive signs of learning after the third or fourth attempt, when the time taken to complete the maze suddenly decreases and the number of mistakes becomes negligible. It may well be that the animal completes the maze rapidly on the first attempt. This is a useful source of discussion with the children because they must realize that it was chance and could not be the result of learning. There is great disappointment if after an initial 'good' time, the time taken to complete the maze for the second attempt seems unduly long. Here the animal is really exploring. To watch this happening is exciting for the children and so far no experiment has yet produced meaningless results. The times have decreased significantly from about five minutes to four seconds, and mistakes from ten to nought. The experiments can be run at twenty-four hour intervals and results compared. If learning had taken place on the previous day one would expect the time taken and the number of mistakes to be much lower on the second day. This is a simple hypothesis which the children will make and which can be readily tested. Invariably the hypothesis holds true, but even if it does not there is then the subsequent need to find out why and this can lead to future experiments.

One group of eight year old children were very excited with one rat which had performed to a very high standard, until, unfortunately, she had stopped to groom herself on the ninth time. This, they considered, ruined their otherwise perfect results and they therefore conveniently excluded the ninth attempt from their final graphs. This desire to achieve 'good' results led to an interesting discussion about what results were, and to their realization that a scientist can only report on what is actually observed and that the verification of the hypothesis must be subject to the results and not vice versa.

Shape preference

The question of whether or not the animals have a 'solid' preference was raised in an earlier experiment on exploring. This can also be extended to shape. The number of shapes used can be limited or extended. The experiment can be carried out in the 'control' cage and the shapes cut out of a wall of card with a reward placed on the opposite side to the animal. This arrangement was the basis of an experiment carried out by some eight year olds and their first choice comprised a square, a circle and a triangle. In order to fit the shapes into the control cage they were cut out of a plain piece of card which fitted across the cage, each shape having a width of six centimetres. The size is unimportant and will depend on the cage size but it was a constant factor in all of these experiments.

Some of the children involved were very able mathematicians and soon realized that although all of the shapes had the same width, they did not share the same surface area. At the completion of the first stage, this small group of children embarked on a further study of the three original shapes but allowed each an equal surface area. To create a triangle with an area equal to that of a square was relatively simple but problems arose with the circle. They knew that the square had an area of 36cm². They needed to know how to find the area of a circle. It meant introducing π and as they were not equipped with log tables or a calculator the measurements were very approximate, but finally they agreed upon a radius of 3.5cm. Their results showed a tendency to prefer the triangle when all shapes had an equal area and they carried out the same logical steps that they had previously followed with the three basic shapes to come to this tentative conclusion.

The procedure with the basic three shapes was interesting for several reasons. First, there was the need, as always, to try to ensure some degree of control through the use of the standard cage. A reward of sunflower seeds was placed opposite the animal to encourage it to go through the hole and a time limit of five minutes was placed on each animal. During the course of the experiments some fascinating results began to emerge but one noticeable feature was that the choice of the animal did not seem to be affected by a reward. The possibility thus arose of removing the reward although this was rejected because the children could see that the experiment would have been modified and it would therefore be more difficult to compare the results.

Developing the experiment
In this experiment, four animals were used—two rats and two gerbils. The original order of the holes was square, circle, triangle. All four animals appeared to like the square. Could a definitive statement be made, therefore, that the favourite shape of the animals was a square? The children might agree to this but with a little encouragement might also suggest that the animals did not prefer that shape but preferred that particular side of the cage. The next step soon became apparent. The shapes must be changed around. A clockwise direction was agreed upon and so the new order became circle, triangle and square. In terms of control, the only change in the experiment was the position of the holes. It was the shape which the children wished to study, it was that which had moved. Rather excitingly, it was again the square which the animals seemed to prefer. The final step obviously had to be to change the position of the shapes for a final time. The last order was therefore triangle, square, circle. The square was still the most popular choice for all animals but what was significant from this last experiment was the reduction in the number of times the animals actually went through the holes. From this series of three experiments it appeared that the square was the favourite shape, but it also appeared that the animals would go through the shape more readily if the square was close to the wall. This behavioural trait confirms what has already been discovered concerning wall-seeking.

The next two stages were suggested by children and gave yet more information on the character and behaviour of animals. The first suggestion recognized that there was a definite shape preference and also recognized there was possibly a positional preference. The idea was very simple but showed a ready understanding. Three squares of equal size were to be placed in the cage and a record kept each time an animal passed through a numbered square. From the evidence already acquired, it appeared that the animals would prefer the outside of the cage. It was a hypothesis scientifically tested and the results quite dramatically confirmed it. In fact, the two gerbils during their five minutes in the cage did not pass through the central square at all.

The second suggestion related to the other work on equal surface area that was happening at the time. This experiment was to retain the basic square and to try to find out whether the animals had a favourite size of square. The number of different sizes that could be offered to the animals was infinite, but simply because of the size of the original control cage the children limited themselves to three squares with sides 6cm, 8cm and 10cm respectively. Once again the experiment needed three stages in order to move the shapes around and it became quite apparent that the larger square with sides of 10cm was definitely the animals' favourite.

This was the stage at which this particular group of children left this series of experiments but possibilities were beginning to open up on other shapes, on comparative areas of shapes and position of shapes. Depending on the number of animals kept, there are obvious possibilities involving sex differences. The list is exhaustive but it is important to realize that there is no final stage to be arrived at, rather that each new experiment raises questions to be answered by further experiments.

Colour preference

Once the apparent favourite shape of the animals has been established, a natural extension of this line of thought is to discover whether the animals have a favourite colour. The choice of colour is an entirely individual matter. Two alternatives spring to mind: either black and white or the primary colours. The children could be allowed to suggest their own alternatives or to choose between the above. If time permits, two parallel experiments can be conducted. For the purposes of this chapter, I shall only talk about our experiment with primary colours.

The experiment was set up in the 'control' cage. A cardboard sheet was placed halfway along the cage and three squares cut out measuring 6cm. This time, however, three compartments were made using cardboard, and three separate but identical rewards offered. The animals were allowed five minutes each in the cage and the children recorded each time an animal went through a particular coloured hole. On the first attempt, the order of the colours was red, yellow and blue. Two rats, two mice and two gerbils were used. In one of the previous experiments on positional preference using three plain squares, the children had noticed that the animals preferred to remain close to the edges and that they rarely passed through the central hole. If this behavioural trait was consistent it would probably affect the result of the new experiment. Therefore, the children's original hypothesis was that if the animals had a favourite colour, it would not be apparent from this experiment because the position of the hole was the overriding factor which would determine their choice. In the light of their former experiences, it seemed a reasonable hypothesis.

Having run the six animals through the experiment the results confounded the children's expectations because red appeared significantly to be the favourite choice. Following on from the series of previous experiments, the next step was immediately realized. It was important now to change the position of the colours to test whether or not red was really a positive choice rather than random chance. It also necessitated the rejection of the original hypothesis and the formulation of a new one. Based on the results obtained, the children now unanimously expected the animals to choose red the greater number of times irrespective of its position. The new position of the colours was yellow, blue and red. Imagine the dismay when, after all the animals had completed five minutes each in the cage and the results compared, they found that not red but yellow appeared significantly more popular. This resulted in the second hypothesis being rejected and a third being formulated. It was beginning to become quite apparent that there was no colour preference, nor the positional preference originally expected (both outside edges equally), but the animals seemed to prefer the coloured hole closest to the left hand side of the cage. The final experiment involved the third change of position for the colours so that the new order was blue, red and yellow. This time, with growing confidence, the children believed that blue would be the favourite choice, not because of its colour but because of its position: closest to the left-hand wall of the cage. This proved to be correct and the conclusion to this experiment was that the animals did not appear to have a favourite colour amongst those offered but did appear to have a distinct preference for the left-hand side of the cage.

Left or right orientation

This final experiment suggests itself as the natural extension of the last one. Although the control was good in the previous experiment and the results quite definite, it had been an experiment to test for colour preference and there had been three possible choices. What was needed to test the new hypothesis—that the animals had a left sided preference—was an entirely new experiment that offered the animals equal choice between left and right. The way this was set up was quite simple. The 'control' cage was used and two identical dishes containing identical rewards placed in the left-hand corner of the cage and the far right-hand corner of the cage. The animals were placed at the other end in a spot which exactly marked the centre. The distance to each dish was exactly the same and the otherwise empty cage offered exactly the same 'environment' whichever way the animal chose to go. It would have been a fitting conclusion to the series of experiments if the results had proved definitely that the animals had either a left or right sided orientation, and the children's hypothesis had naturally been that the animals would take the reward from the left side dish the greater number of times, but no such definite results appeared. The choice was greater for the left-hand dish but only marginally so. Future experiments that the children will carry out will look even more closely into ways of studying animal behaviour and try to create new situations where the degree of control is greater, so that they can add more information to the already large amount of statistical evidence they have gathered about the animals they keep at school.

Conclusions

Experimental work using animals is very rewarding for children and teachers. Anyone interested in embarking on a programme should remember, though, the time required for such work. Time will be needed to clean the animals regularly. Dinner time is very useful for this task as it does not impinge upon 'academic' time. Time will be needed to handle the animals daily and again, dinner times, break times, before and after school do not take up 'teaching time'. What about the time required to carry out the actual experiments? Much of the teaching time in our school is based on an integrated curriculum and the children, therefore, have blocks of time, unrestricted by a bell signifying the end of a lesson, to complete such work. This does not, however, restrict teachers working in more traditional schools from carrying out such work. None of the experiments suggested took longer than five minutes to complete. If a number of animals are to be used, then a number of experiments could be run simultaneously. In a thirty or forty minute session this still allows for the work to be recorded on tally charts or bar graphs and for the experiment to be written up.

In whichever type of school the teacher is working, the longer one has to carry out such work, the more rewarding the results will be, not in terms of the experiments but in terms of the interest of the children, in their attitudes, in their learning and in their motivation. If any further justification is needed, the following eloquent piece of work should provide it:

> The rat is a friend to us with that beautiful look in her eyes it makes you nearly want to cry. She will be leaving us soon. I will never forget that shine in her eyes and that hood over her face. She has got a loving look in her face. Those ears that lovely pink and her white back. And that long tail of yours and your soft whiskers you used to cuddle in my

jumper. I feel sorry Rat. She will die of cancer. I'll never forget you. But you had a good life with us. You'll die peacefully. That's the way it goes in nature.

Stephen Andrews, 8 years old

This was written on the death from cancer of a very old hooded rat. The children watched the swellings of the lymph glands increase over a number of weeks, as the cancer grew. They treated her with care and respect and love as they saw her dying. It was a profound lesson.

She was a friendly rat, as Stephen has so ably told us. Animals do provide a powerful force for the moral, social and emotional development of young children. If a teacher wishes to have animals in the classroom for no other reason, that alone should be valid justification for their presence.

6
Developing outdoor resources for primary science

Abbey Park First School is located in Pershore, a small town within the rural setting of the Vale of Evesham.

The school has approximately 200 boys and girls on roll with ages ranging from 5 to 9 years, and a teaching establishment of head + 7. There is no formal timetable for science, the subject forming part of the project/topic work in the lower part of the school, and environmental studies with the older children occupying about 50 per cent of their weekly programme. All staff teach science in some form each term, and one member of staff acts as school adviser for the subject.

6

Developing outdoor resources for primary science

John Devine

Not all schools are fortunate enough to have spacious surroundings, but many schools do have areas of land on site which could be used to create outdoor resources for science without the loss of playing space and without too much expense(**1**).

On the piece of land which has been developed at Abbey Park First School there are hutches for male and female rabbits and a very secure enclosure for ducks and ducklings. The children learn a great deal from caring for and observing these animals and especially from seeing them rear their young. In addition to the animals, the area has on it a variety of features and habitats for plant and animal life which provide an opportunity for observing, recording, measuring, investigating, testing, discussing, and questioning which can be followed up in the classroom in a number of ways. Included in these are six main resources.

1 A wild area

This is a mound composed of bricks, stones and compost buried under leaf litter and top soil. It occupies an area of some $10m^2$ and rises to a height of about 1m. The purpose of this mound is to provide a wild, unweeded area in which children can search for slugs, snails, and small creatures which inhabit such dumping grounds(**2**). Specimens can be examined, recorded and drawn in the field or kept in the classroom for longer studies of their habits using simple vivariums made from glass or plastic fish tanks(**3**). Some of the compost, stone, etc. from which the animals are removed can be placed in the tank and the material kept damp with a little water. Slugs, snails and a wide variety of other minibeasts can be kept successfully in this way for short periods of study.

One investigation carried out by nine year olds was to see whether or not a snail's journey could be recorded on paper. After various suggestions had been pursued, the task was accomplished by covering the fresh trail with paste and then sprinkling this with glitter.

Creating such a wild area is not difficult if the children save garden rubbish. The local council may be a source of unwanted top soil, leaf litter, logs, bricks and stones. If the resultant pile is planted with a few shrubs it will not be unsightly.

The natural colonization of the mound with wild seeds and roots from such plants as nettles, thistles and dandelions is an interesting long-term study to undertake with children. The periodic count of different plants, their indentification in reference books and discussions as to how they might have arrived on the mound are all worthwhile features of such a study. Weeds should, if possible, be left to flower and seed, in order to nourish as wide a variety of animal life on the mound as possible. If it is not possible to make a mound, an alternative is to create a wild patch at ground level by removing turf, etc. and leaving the area roped-off to see which plants establish themselves, adding perhaps a few logs and large stones.

The presence of decaying material in such an area can lead the children into discussions about the slow changes that take place when the plants die. They can look for moulds and other evidence of decay such as the presence of leaf 'skeletons'. Simple investigations can be made into which conditions most favour the rotting of leaves. Do the ones on top of the pile decay quicker than those buried beneath? If the pile is forked over every week in one area, how does this compare with another which is left undisturbed? Does regular watering make any difference? Can the children draw any conclusions about the process of decay and the conditions that encourage its acceleration? By washing off some of the decaying material in a small bucket and examining the water with hand lens or microscope, can the children find any evidence of animal life which is helping to break down the compost(**4,5**)?

2 Trees

These include types that demonstrate some of the differences and similarities which children can be made aware of when studying trees(**6**). There are many advantages to having a good variety of trees on site. It only takes a short time to reach them, they are accessible throughout the year and no one's permission is required to collect specimens or to set up experiments which involve the trees themselves. Collections can be made of bark-rubbings, leaves, buds, flowers, fruit and seeds as the seasons progress, and the skills of tree-identification can be fostered as part of a wider study of trees and wood. This gives valuable experience in looking for pattern, like and unlike features, as well as investigating hardness, colour, grain-pattern, density and consequent uses of different types of timber(**7, 8**).

The study of trees can introduce children to simple ideas of conservation and balance in nature. Most young children will readily tell us that birds and squirrels depend largely on trees but, by holding an outstretched white sheet under a low bough and tapping the bough with a heavy stick, it is often possible to collect a suprisingly wide variety of small creatures which can also be seen to be dependent upon the tree in some way, as well as providing food for the birds. If the exercise is repeated at different times of the year, the results lead to even more fruitful discussion. Children can begin to understand that some birds migrate because their food supply is affected by seasonal changes, rather than ascribing migration to 'the cold'.

3 Tree gardens

It is to be hoped that children will develop a respect for trees as a vital part of the environment. One good way of encouraging this is to provide them with an opportunity to grow their own trees from seed. Through such experience, children will begin to appreciate the time trees take to grow and the difficulty of replacing them if they are damaged. To this end, we have established simple tree gardens based on a system introduced in Germany during the 1930s by Adolf Dunemann using what are known as Dunemann bins. The method is very simple and cheap and can be tackled in any primary school, even where space is very limited, using old sinks, deep-walled tyres or bins made from wood.

Constructing a Dunemann bin
The container needs to be deep enough to hold 22cm–24cm (9in) of compost and the ideal material to use is well rotted leaf mould collected from beneath conifer trees. Permission to do this should always be obtained as trees are often carefully protected, particularly in parks.

Having established the bin, corner posts are used to support a roof or canopy at a height of about 46cm (18in) above the surface of the leaf-mould, allowing space for the trees to grow. This canopy can be constructed of fine netting or laths of timber secured to two side rails in 'hit-and-miss' style so that about 50% of the overhead light is cut out, thereby simulating forest floor conditions. The fine netting has the same effect. The whole structure must be covered with strawberry netting to keep birds, mice and cats away from the seeds and seedlings.

Siting and filling the bin
The bin is best sited in a sheltered north-facing position, perhaps against a wall but not under trees. A water supply will be necessary and this is worth bearing in mind if there is any choice in the matter of positioning the bin, or bins. At the filling stage, it is best to remove stones and twigs from the conifer litter and sieve out the finer particles to use as a top layer in which the seeds are sown and covered.

Seeding the bin
Seeds, either purchased or collected from cones or from under deciduous trees in the autumn and stored in a cool, dry place are sown in the spring. The faster-growing varieties such as larch and chestnut can reach 15cm

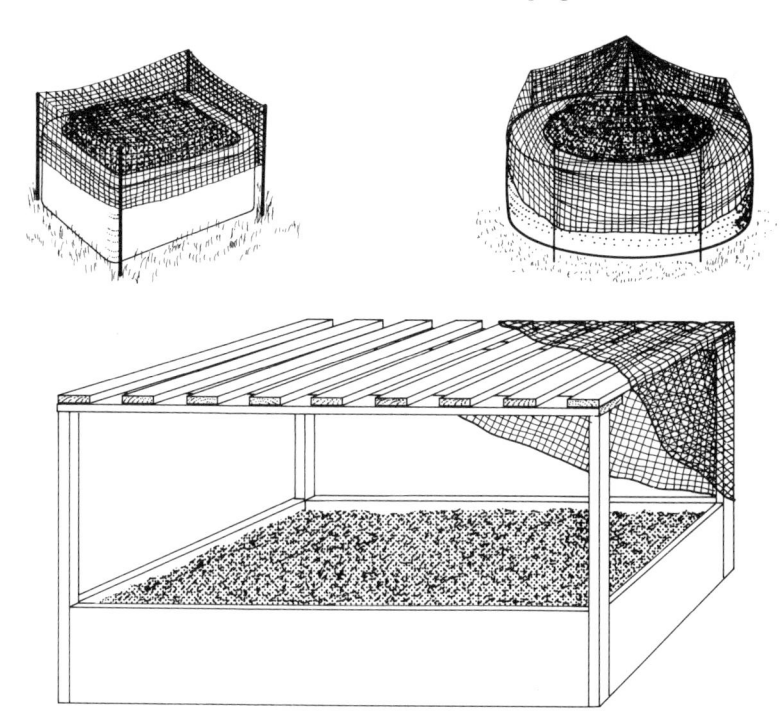

Figure 19 Constructing a Dunemann Bin
  a) Using an old sink
  b) Using a deep-walled tyre
  c) Using wooden boards

(6in) in height by the autumn of the same year. The seeds should be sown in rows about 50mm (2in) apart, covered first with the leaf-mould and then with a fine grit obtainable from any pet shop. This prevents the wind from blowing away the top layer. Use labels *and* a diagrammatic record at sowing time to ensure that information about the names, numbers and position of seeds is not lost.

The bin must not be allowed to dry out. Weeds are best pinched out while still young so that disturbance of the trees is kept to a minimum. After two years, or one for the fast-growing varieties, the trees are removed from the bin during the winter months, taking care not to damage the fibrous roots. These can be wrapped in polythene bags to prevent drying out. Even a small bin can produce a large number of seedlings and there is much to be gained from establishing two small bins, one in the first year and another in the second, so that they can be used in rotation. We have grown conifers, rather than deciduous trees, because of the faster growth-rate of many varieties. Scots pine, larch, thuja and

Norway spruce (Christmas tree), have been germinated, the latter being particularly appealing to the children.

I would recommend the Dunemann bin idea to any school initiating regular work involving trees because it brings a very rewarding and interesting dimension to the work. The value of making models is recognized as an excellent aid to children's learning, and in a sense, the Dunemann bin is a model of the forest floor, recreating the main requirements of tree seed germination and providing an excellent basis for discussion and study which can be linked to a woodland visit.

4 A weather station

This is rather a grand title for a few simple pieces of apparatus on the area which are used for measurements, recordings and predictions about the weather. The value of involving children in keeping weather records cannot, in my view, be over-stated. It provides opportunities for the careful reading of a dial or scale and helps to develop knowledge and accuracy about making and using graphs and tables. Above all, it contributes in a very meaningful way to teaching about the weather and seasons.

The instruments which I would recommend include the following:

A rain gauge
This is a container calibrated in ml for measuring daily rainfall. For cheapness one can use a jam jar and measuring cylinder, but a proper rain gauge, which will give results that are standardized and can be compared with official readings from real weather stations, is not very expensive and worth having. Most educational suppliers produce school models.

A maximum/minimum thermometer
This is examined each day at the same hour and gives the highest and lowest temperatures reached during the preceeding 24 hours. After each reading, the thermometer is reset and those designed for primary schools are quite easy to use. Ideally, the thermometer should be housed inside a Stevenson's screen, which is a white-painted cabinet having slatted sides allowing the air to pass over the thermometer bulb and yet protecting it from direct sun, wind and rain. However, such screens are expensive to buy and any wooden, slatted box which can be painted white to achieve similar conditions within, will be adequate for demonstrating the principle of the screen.

Records of both maximum and minimum temperatures can be displayed on the same graph to give children opportunity to understand the idea of a range of temperature. If records are continued over the terms, this gives great meaning to the teacher's demands for care and accuracy and also provides wider scope for analysis of temperatures

Developing outdoor resources 87

throughout the different periods. The occurrence of sub-zero temperatures offers a very natural link for teaching children about freezing point and the existence of positive and negative numbers.

An anemometer

This is a rotating device which spins in the wind so that the revolutions per minute can be counted in order to compare day-to-day wind force. The r.p.m. can be converted to wind speed, but for younger children it is sufficient to establish a simple scale of wind-force. This can be done by noting the r.p.m. on a very windy day and dividing the figure by four or five, establishing a number of ranges of r.p.m., for example, 0–10, 10–20, 20–30 and so on. The children can be introduced to the official Beaufort Wind Scale(**9**) and make up one for their own weather station related to the school site, e.g. 0–10 r.p.m. ... trees near our classroom are still; 10–20 r.p.m. ... crisp packets blow along school playground, etc.

The exercise of constructing with the children home-made anemometers from scrap materials is worthwhile, since it helps them to appreciate the workings of the anemometer. However, it is not easy to make a really strong one and it is worth considering the purchase of a commercially produced schools' model to avoid the frustration of having the project interrupted by the failure or breakage of a home-made anemometer. The apparatus should be securely mounted on a tall pole and ideally should be well away from buildings.

Other aspects of weather study which can be included without any expenditure and which give further practice in observing, recording and predicting are as follows:

cloud types: recognition of main types and associated weather
cloud cover: readings expressed as a percentage or fraction of the sky
visibility: established by determining a number of landmarks seen from the school at different distances, e.g. $\frac{1}{2}$km, 1km, $1\frac{1}{2}$km, etc.
wind direction: either using a compass or home-made wind vane and recording results on a 'wind rose' which is a graph

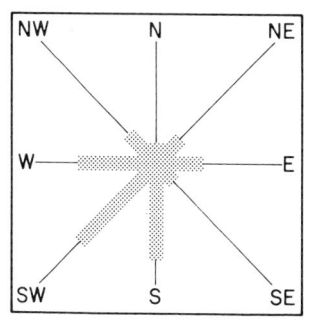

Figure 20 A wind rose graph showing dominant wind direction

radiating out along the main eight points of the compass, thus depicting dominant wind direction over a given number of days

5 Two bee hives

These stand in a secluded corner of the area separated from the nearby buildings by a tall hedge through which the bees will not fly. In front of the hives is a screen of fine nylon netting. This also forces the bees up so that they come and go well above head-height while children watch beekeeping demonstrations through the netting in safety. Small groups also enter the apiary itself and take an active part in studying the progress of the two colonies of bees. For this they need to wear a bee veil, gloves and long trousers, taking care to protect wrists and ankles.

In the wild state, bees live predominantly in hollow trees. In the darkness of these cavities they construct honey combs using the hexagonal pattern with which most people are familiar. Inside the cells of this beeswax comb, food is stored in the form of honey and pollen, and the queen bee lays eggs which hatch into milky-white grubs. These are then fed by 'nurse' bees until the grubs fill the cells, at which point the cells are capped and the larvae pupate. Eventually, the emergent young bees break their way out of the cappings to be fed until they are ready to play their part in the work of the colony, the whole process having taken 21 days from the laying of the eggs (16 for queen bees).

The beekeeper provides the bees with small wooden frames in which they build their honey comb, each hive containing between ten and twelve frames. In the summer, and if the flow of nectar from flowers has been sufficient, the bees produce surplus stores of honey in extra frames which the hopeful beekeeper also provides. A special screen called a queen-excluder prevents the laying of eggs in these frames, and it is from here that the harvest is collected(**10**).

The activities of bees and their role in the environment is of great interest and educational value to children. The keeping of bees in primary schools is less difficult and certainly much safer than is generally thought and one good way to start is by establishing an observation hive. This is a case containing just two or three frames of bees with their queen, which can be observed in complete safety through the glass sides of the case. Children will see all the activities of the full-sized hive, but on a smaller scale, the observation hive being installed in the classroom or outside in summer. Anyone prepared to look into the possibilities of beekeeping in schools will almost certainly be surprised to discover how much free help and advice is available. This applies throughout the British Isles since beekeeping is not an exclusively rural activity. The address of your nearest beekeeping association is obtainable from the General Secretary of the British Beekeepers' Association(**11**). In addition, many counties have full-time or part-time Beekeeping Officers and every County Education Office should have a member of staff who can give advice about the nearest organization that offers information and courses for beginners.

Figure 21 The ponds

6 The ponds

As can be seen above, we have two ponds which are of similar concrete construction. One is enclosed with chain-link fencing for the ducks mentioned at the beginning of this chapter. The larger one, in the foreground, is a 'natural' pond which is intended as a model of the sort that used to be so common in the countryside(**12**). As a resource for science teaching with young children, the potential of such a pond is considerable.

I shall set out below how we planned for and constructed our 'natural' pond. If, however, you feel that developing this particular outdoor resource is too complicated for your school site, the discussion beginning on p. 93 concerning plant and animal life in the pond, the food chain, and most importantly, *using a pond*, will be helpful for school visits to environmental centres or parks.

Planning for a concrete pond

Size
Whereas many potential pond-diggers might hesitate at the suggestion that their pond be more than two or three square metres in area, my

advice would be to build it bigger if possible. I say this for several reasons. The result of investigating a very small pond, even with only half a class, is that there simply is not enough pond to go round. Because the children can reach every corner of a small pond, the animals living in it have no sanctuary at times of dipping. Pond life can become over-disturbed and may fail to survive. Should a small pond be the only practical possibility, it would be strongly advisable to restrict greatly the occasions on which it is dipped, and the number of children involved each time.

Shape
Since a concrete liner is virtually permanent, it pays to plan the shape very carefully. There is no one particular design which has great advantages over others and no reason why the children should not be involved in making drawings and helping the teacher to arrive at a shape for the pond which is both pleasing to the eye and practicable to build. Natural ponds tend not to have sharp corners, and in any case, a curve is easier to lay in concrete.

An island
Having an island means that the plan can include long narrow stretches of water across which the children can reach easily and safely for dipping. If the island is left undisturbed and a few logs and rocks are put on it as well as shrubby willows and dogswood, shelter will be created for animals such as frogs and toads and make the pond look more natural.

The cross-section of the pond
There are three important factors to consider as far as the cross-section is concerned:

i) There needs to be sufficient depth of water in one area of the pond to protect animal life during periods when there is thick ice on the surface. A depth of at least 60cm (2ft) is advised.

ii) Different plants prefer different depths(**13, 14**), and if examples of these are to be established, hedges can be included in the design to support containers for these plants.

iii) The edges of the pond are best kept gently sloping and shallow so children who step into the water do not become too wet or distressed. These shallow areas provide an ideal bird bath, a safe drinking place for animals and a good observation area for studying any pond life which comes to the edge, such as snails and tadpoles.

Marking out the shape of the pond
Once the shape and size of the pond have been decided upon, the next stage is to mark this out on to the surface of the ground. Sawdust (or sand)

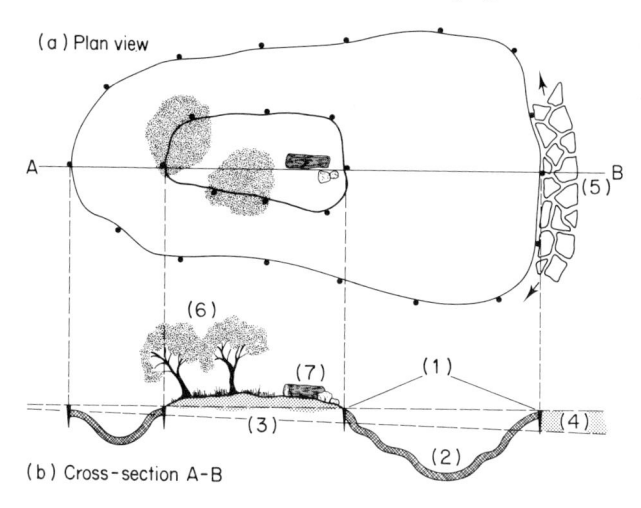

Figure 22 Construction of the concrete pond

a) Plan view

b) Cross section A-B

Key to diagram:
(1) wooden pegs giving horizontal level (later removed)
(2) concrete liner with shelves at different depths
(3) original ground level before commencing digging out
(4) spoil from digging-out used to raise low areas
(5) pathway of broken slabs sunk into ground for ease of moving
(6) shrubs planted on the island to give useful shade over water
(7) logs and rocks offer cover for animal life

is a useful aid at this point since a raised line made of it shows up well. Mistakes and alterations can easily be brushed out with a broom until the final design is achieved.

An allowance of some 10cm (4in) must be made for the thickness of the concrete liner so the shape marked out on the ground will need to be that much bigger all round than the final inner surface of the liner; and the island, if there is to be one, that much smaller. Consequently the markings on the ground will give an exaggerated impression of the pond's surface area.

Checking for levels

Water has a nasty habit of lying perfectly level and there is nothing more frustrating and embarrassing than filling the completed pond only to find the water over-flowing at one end while the other is still dry. To overcome this problem it is necessary, before digging starts, to check the lie of the land around the perimeter of the pond and also any island with a spirit level. One can ensure that the edges of the concrete liner will be on the same horizontal plane by levelling the tops of wooden pegs hammered into the ground at $\frac{1}{2}$m intervals all the way round the perimeter markings (see Fig. 22). The concrete will be laid up to the top of these pegs. If the first peg is hammered in at a low point on the ground markings, this may result in the need to dig out higher areas creating unwanted banks sloping down to the pond. It is therefore better to place the first peg at the highest point on the ground markings and build up low areas using soil dug out as the hole progresses. Any such raised areas should be firmly trodden down, and it may be necessary to re-mark them before trimming the final edge of the hole. The finished pond will therefore be at ground level all the way round and any surrounding banks will slope away from the water. This makes access easier and the laying of a surrounding pathway feasible (see Fig. 22).

Digging the hole for the pond
This operation will vary in difficulty according to the state of the soil, but it is worthwhile having a pick-axe at hand to remove bricks and stones which tend to be uncovered near buildings. Since digging out is heavy work, it is as well to enlist some help with the task. Apart from building up low areas as stated, the soil from the hole can be used to create low relief on an island, to make a raised flower or herb bed elsewhere on site or to create the wild area described at the beginning of this chapter. *Over-deepen* the hole to allow for the liner.

Laying the concrete liner
Concrete is a mixture of sand and gravel with cement powder and water. The sand and gravel can be obtained in units of cubic metres and the cement is supplied in 50kg (1cwt) bags. It is necessary to add a waterproofing solution to the concrete when it is being mixed, and this normally comes in one gallon containers. These materials are obtainable from builders' merchants but it is worth appealing for donated materials among any contacts which the school might have in the building trade.

Where to mix the concrete
Since transporting full wheelbarrows of mixed concrete is very heavy work, it pays to have the materials dumped as near as possible to the site of the pond. If a hard surface is not available, suitable boards should be laid down for dumping and mixing.

Polythene sheeting
It is necessary to line the hole with polythene sheeting before concreting begins. This prevents the concrete from mixing with the soil and slows down the drying process to prevent cracking. Old chicken wire or similar material can be laid on top of the polythene where the sides of the pond slope steeply. This will help support the concrete while it sets and will act as reinforcement.

Mixing the Concrete: Ratios and quantities
A ratio of four parts sand and gravel to one part cement will give a strong enough bond for the pond liner. Waterproofing solution is added according to the manufacturer's instructions. Enough water should be added, a little at a time, to create a pudding-like mixture, and the use of a cement mixer is highly recommended if one can be borrowed or hired for a day, since concrete mixing by hand is *very* heavy work. Once again, an adequate labour force is essential to ensure continuous laying once concreting has begun.

It will be necessary to calculate the approximate amount of sand and gravel and the number of bags of cement that will be required. Allowing for a thickness of at least 10cm (4in) for the liner and estimating the surface area of the hole will provide the figures necessary for calculating the approximate volume of mix required. One cubic metre of mix would make about ten square metres of liner, but extra must be allowed for thicker areas.

Thickness of liner for a 60cm (2ft) deep pond
One should aim for a thickness of at least 10cm (4in) when laying the concrete, allowing a little more for shoulders, which need to be strong. The liner must not become thin at the edges of the pond since it is here that people will be standing and walking and where exposure to the elements will be greatest.

Ready-mixed concrete
There is no reason why this should not be used if funds are available. In this case, the waterproofing solution is added by the manufacturer. However, it is essential to have enough helpers at hand to lay the liner quickly before the pile of ready-mixed concrete begins to harden. This can be a very serious problem in hot, dry weather.

Filling and stocking the pond

The process of filling the pond with a hose-pipe offers an opportunity for some useful investigations. How long will it take? How many litres will be required and how can we measure this?

Once the pond is filled, it should be left for a few days before any plant or animal life is introduced. At this stage, the children can begin making recordings of any animals such as birds and insects that adopt or visit the pond, and also note any fluctuations in the water-level by making a scale of marks on the concrete edge of the pond. On more than one occasion, we have mistaken high evaporation rates for evidence that the pond was leaking!

Introducing plant life
With concrete beneath the water, there will be considerable limitation to the amount of plant life that the pond can support. Nevertheless, it is important to try to maintain enough to ensure a healthy, well-balanced pond which provides sufficient oxygen, food, shelter and shade for a wide range of animal life(**5, 13**).

Floating plants such as water starwort, frog-bit, duck weed and water soldier require no soil for their roots and will offer shade and shelter for small animal life beneath their leaves. Too much sunlight can encourage the rapid spread of slimy green algae which becomes a problem once it takes a hold. At the same time, a check must be kept on the spread of plants like duckweed which can increase very rapidly and create too much shade.

Plants which have leaves at the surface but roots on the bottom, such as water-lilies and broad-leaved pond weed, can be established using home-made chicken wire baskets to hold soil for their roots. These baskets can be weighted to keep them in position.

Other plants which remain submerged, such as curled pond weed, Canadian pond weed and hornwort may be introduced in the same way. Additionally, large polythene or fertilizer bags can be filled with debris from a thriving pond in summer and the material emptied onto the bottom of the new pond. This will provide for minute pond life which is the basis of the pond's food 'pyramid'.

Introducing animal life
The debris described above will have among it many forms of microscopic animal life as well as shrimp, water lice and other slightly larger creatures. Since healthy, unpolluted ponds are not as common as they were, it may be necessary to consult your local wildlife associations or park keepers in order to locate a good source of pond life. Animals which can be used to stock the pond include the following:

fish: stickleback and minnow
amphibians: common frog, common toad, smooth newt and crested newt
animals with shells: freshwater winkle, ramshorn snail, pond snail and lake limpet
insects: water boatmen (two types, one of which swims on its back), water stick insect, water scorpion, whirligig beetle, diving beetle and pond skater
insect larva: gnat, midge, blood worm, caddis fly, stone fly, alder fly and dragon fly

The food 'pyramid'(**5, 13**)
This is a term which describes the way in which large numbers of microscopic animals provide food for fewer larger species which, in their turn, support smaller numbers of even bigger animals. At the base of this

'pyramid' are the minute plant-eaters and at the top, the frogs and birds. It is important to bear this food pyramid in mind when stocking the pond and to discuss its implications with the children. For example, the new pond may only be able to support one breeding pair of frogs, whereas large numbers of pond snails can be introduced fairly safely.

Using a pond

Pond-side observations
Children should be encouraged to approach the pond slowly and quietly if they hope to see much activity round the edge. Which animals can be seen, and what are they doing? Are they hovering, flying about, skating on the surface, swimming or crawling on the bottom? Which are solitary and which are in groups? How quickly do they move? Do they move at the same speed all the time?

Pond dipping
Great care must be taken to ensure that this is done properly or the pond will suffer considerable damage and disturbance. It is worth buying or making a few good-quality pond nets with light canvas rather than open mesh netting, otherwise the children will find it impossible to collect minute pond life, and some of the larger specimens may be damaged when the children try to free them from the netting.

To dip the pond, children should reach out over the surface gently and drag the net steadily down and in towards their feet, twisting it up as it reaches the bank. The spare hand is used to raise the canvas from beneath the net while it is still in the water to inspect its contents. This method minimizes the disturbance to the pond's surface and safeguards whatever is in the net. A bucket of pond water should be at hand on the bank for holding any specimens which are transferred to the classroom for closer study. A spoon, a pair of tweezers and an eye dropper are useful tools for this task. Water boatmen can bite!

Classroom follow-up
Shallow white plastic trays containing 4–5cm of clean pond water provide excellent containers for observing pond life in the classroom for short periods.

Children experience great delight in catching something interesting in the pond, but almost as much pleasure is derived from *identifying* the animal in a reference book. Time should be allowed for detailed and accurate drawings made from first-hand observations rather than by tracing pictures in books, since the former encourages much more attention to detail.

Written descriptions will also be a part of follow-up work and the children can be given guidelines to help them organize their thoughts:

Animals with legs: How many pairs of legs are there? Are they the same size? Are the legs jointed? How are the legs used?

Animals with shells: Is there one shell or two? Is the shell coiled or fan-like? What markings are there? Does the animal come out of the shell?

Animals with jointed bodies: How many body segments are there? Are they the same size? How do the joints move? Are there legs on all segments?

Animals with wings: How many pairs of wings are there? Do the wings remain open? Has the animal feelers?

Fish: How many fins are on the back? How many on the sides? Do all the fins move? Has the fish any markings? Can the gills be seen?

Movement: How does the animal move? Does it move on the surface, through the water or on the bottom? What body parts make it move?

Breathing: Can a mouth be seen? Does the animal appear to need to rise to the surface to breathe?

Together with these first-hand observations, the children can find out about the animals' feeding, breeding and life cycles from books, thus expanding upon the valuable experience offered by the school pond.

The final step is to *return* the animals to their natural habitat.

Conclusions

The school environment, whether inner-city, suburban, town or rural, can be used creatively as a valuable resource for primary science. Children can learn a great deal from studying plants and animals and their habitats, whether in a small patch just outside the classroom, or in a substantial piece of ground populated by a large variety of flora and fauna.

Developing outdoor resources for primary science can result in children gaining a respect for and understanding of the complex natural world of which they are a part. Using outdoor resources can be as simple as systematically looking at the weather, or as complex as constructing a pond, and is within the financial grasp of all primary schools.

7
Science for younger children

Holmer Infants' School was built in 1900 and is situated in the City of Hereford. At present it has over 100 pupils aged 4+ to 7 years.

It is the policy of the school to incorporate science into the curriculum from the earliest stages. Later, science can be included in a project or used as the central core. If the latter, then a whole morning per week is used over half a term with related language, number and craft work following the scientific experiments.

7

Science for younger children

Sheila James and Penny Redshaw

Science for younger children exists very much within their own familiar environment. Situations occur within all good teaching of this age group where pupils' potential can be identified and the processes of science developed. This needs appropriate planning, the posing of relevant questions and the encouragement of the child's natural curiosity.

Accordingly, no fresh experience will be introduced in this chapter for starting science in the earlier years of formal schooling. Instead, familiar topics will be discussed to show how children can be taught a scientific approach and be led to conclusions in a way appropriate to their stage of conceptual development.

It is in this spirit that the inclusion of science in the curriculum for this age group is approached. Five areas, none of them new to the infant scene, are examined to explore their science potential, and the contribution concludes with suggested plans for incorporating four science based topics into a school curriculum.

1 Structured play

Small children involve themselves in many activities where order and sequence can be shown to have importance, not least in imaginative situations as in the Wendy House.

During a 'pretend' day, the dolls get up in the morning and are washed and dressed. The children notice the sequence and can try the effect of reversing it to dressing and washing. The reasons for the necessary order can then be talked about.

Setting the table for dolls' meals involves utensils appropriate to the task. The effects of insufficient and inappropriate tools can be investigated—forks for custard, tumblers for chips. Although the experiments can seem only fun, the smallest children will appreciate the need for the appropriate implement. Different ways of cleaning the Wendy House and its contents can be investigated. A duster, a dry and a wet sponge, warm water and warm soapy water, rain and tap water are possibilities. The clothes can be dried inside, in the classroom by a radiator, outside on a still day, on a windy day or on a hot day to discover conditions best for drying. Where *does* the water go to? Results can be compared with those for the drying of a puddle in the playground after a shower. This can be measured by a chalk mark drawn round at intervals during the day.

Toy shops of sufficient variety—a grocers', a post office, sweet shops and a clothes store all offer plenty of practice in matching, sorting and discrimination.

Constructive play also introduces children to the need for selection, in this case for the best material so that a particular effect can be achieved. Chalk, crayon, charcoal, felt pens, paint, clay, polystyrene and scrap fabrics can be tried for different situations. If collage work is attempted then the concept of texture enters—types and colours of papers, the super-imposition of coloured tissue paper. Wax resist work can be tried and can provide opportunites for questions and reasons.

Sand and water play are well established in the infant world and can be extended to provide real scientific experience. Sand can be examined wet and dry, with the naked eye, with a magnifying glass and with a microscope. Cartons of wet and dry sand can be weighed for comparison and with other materials, e.g. sugar or salt.

Water play introduces the concepts of capacity and volume. Questions can be posed for discussion:

> How many times do we fill the school water jug to fill a bucket?
> How many to fill a bowl?
> How long does it take to fill the jug from a beaker?
> How long for the jug to fill the sink?
> Try various objects in water to see if they sink or float.
> Look at how much of the floating object is on top of the water and how much is underneath.
> Try adding Plasticine to the floating objects. Will they sink now?

Drops of water on different surfaces—cotton wool, rubber, metal, feathers, foil, polystyrene and wood—behave differently. How?

Raindrops can be watched racing down the window—and down other surfaces. Which surface is best—glass, tile, polystyrene or brick? Does a big drop go more or less slowly than a little drop?

All of these activities are happening now in infant classrooms. They are already being used for language development, for mathematics and for art and craft. Their value can be extended to help children make accurate observations and apply reasoned tests to reach intelligent conclusions.

2 Ourselves and our senses

Children have a natural curiosity about themselves that can be channelled to provide opportunites for investigation.

Heights, hand spans, sizes of hands and feet can be compared. Is it the children with the largest hands who have the largest feet? Prints of feet walking, running and hopping can be compared for stride lengths.

Tests can be made on the best way to keep clean; hands can be washed in cold water and in warm water, in both cases with and without soap. Hair can be compared for strength and colour. Plaster casts of teeth can be made of impressions bitten into Plasticine. Teeth for chewing and for biting can be identified. All of these activities provide opportunities to assemble information and to test whether conclusions reached are appropriate.

Different clothing can be tested for effectiveness in providing warmth. 'Dolls' of squeezy bottles with cardboard heads are dressed in different fabrics—cotton, wool, fur or foil—and filled with hot water. The rate of cooling is assessed by feeling the bottles at set intervals. The order in which they cool can be the starting point for discussions on the most appropriate clothing for different weather conditions.

The different clothes worn by children on a rainy day can be the starting point for finding out which fabrics are most appropriate for keeping water out. Samples of materials are stretched over jam jar openings and the passage of a tablespoonful of water through each timed. This can be compared with the rate through the same fabrics which have been moistened before starting. The rate at which samples of different fabrics soak up water can be compared and the best conditions for drying—inside, outside on a heap or pegged on a line, can be discussed. Given the same conditions, do different fabrics take different amounts of time to dry?

All five senses provide opportunities for structured work:

Sight
Eye colours can be compared—each others' and parents'. Can a child find his way around a room with his eyes closed? How do our eyes compare in size and position with those of birds and animals? How do different objects appear from different levels and directions through small and large holes, with magnifying glasses and with microscopes? Which colours are most visible under given conditions?

Look at mirrors, puddles, shiny things. Study images in mirrors placed at angles.

How many colours can be identified in a rainbow? How many colours are needed to paint a rainbow? Look at petrol lying in a puddle and compare the number of colours there with a rainbow.

Hearing
Listen to sounds inside and outside the classroom.
Different sounds can be compared—a twanging ruler, vibrating rubber bands, objects suspended on strings and tapped, and bottles with different volumes of water. Simple percussion instruments can be made based on

results from these tests. High and low notes can be tested for by seeing how long and thick vibrating strings give lower notes than short and thin ones.

Children enjoy making sound travel and realizing the difference if it is made to go through air, through a solid, e.g. a desk or floor, or through water. Telephones can be made with cartons and tins. Which are the best? Does the shape make any difference?

Taste
Select several white (and safe) substances such as sugar, salt, flour, icing sugar, blancmange powder, baking powder, ground rice, dried milk. Place these in small jars. Do they look alike? Do they taste the same? Try them and guess what they are. Things can be the same colour but do not taste the same.

Try other substances—cocoa and cinnamon, vinegar and Coca-Cola. These look the same but do not taste the same.

Smell
Cover plastic containers with foil and poke holes in the foil. Slices of lemon and of orange, pepper, ginger, ground coffee, perfume, etc. in each, will challenge children to identify the unseen objects. Is there any difference if a child has a cold? The smells can be sorted into 'liked' and 'not liked'.

Touch
Work on this sense can be allied to work on texture which is described later in this chapter.

3 Surroundings

Collections of leaves, flowers, twigs, etc. provide valuable observation and discussion points. Grouping of these for shape or colour, number of petals, size, arrangement of twig or stem can help the children to order their thinking. While exploring their surroundings, they are using their senses and developing their language ability.

Indoors, carrot tops can be grown, cress can be cultivated to be eaten later, an avocado stone planted, lemon and orange pips and flower seeds sown, and bulbs planted in soil and in water. Tests can be made on these to show effects of light, dark and water. If there is room outside, children love to have a small patch of garden—perhaps a square of garden alternated with a square of paving slabs to keep their feet dry. They can then experiment with the growing of vegetables and flowers.

4 Interest Tables or corners

Themes suitable for interest tables include:

Round things	Textures	Things that make sounds
Pretty things	Patterns	Seaside things
Shiny things	Coloured things	Moving things

Suitable objects can be brought in by children or by staff. The tables can be class based or in a central position for discussion by more than one class, perhaps in assembly time. It is important that they are well presented, changed regularly and used. Observation of the objects in detail is important—from all angles and with mirrors and magnifiers where appropriate.

5 Themes and projects

Integrated work on a chosen theme covers all aspects of the curriculum. The science content can be specifically extracted as positively as are the basics of language and number or the art and craft. Examples include:

'News' time
For many children the weekly and sometimes daily expectations of a record of events of the day or weekend can be repetitive. If they are encouraged to look for blue or green things, notice the trees or bring food from home to examine under the microscope, then at least their own observations will be more interesting than 'I played with my toys and watched television'.

Popular stories and nursery rhymes:
   Goldilocks and the Three Bears
    a) Three bears—their sizes. Comparisons of other fathers, mothers and children and appropriate beds, chairs and bowls.
    b) Three bowls of porridge—which would cool first?
    c) Three chairs—what weight will large, medium and small models hold?

   Humpty Dumpty Sat on a Wall
    a) Humpty Dumpty—observe and discuss what is inside an egg. Can the broken eggshell be repaired?
    b) Walls—examine walls of different types and construction. Can we build a wall? Try different materials for building and see how strong the walls are.
       Invite a bricklayer to school to demonstrate his craft and let the children try to build a wall.

Television programmes
Many questions and investigations arise from such programmes specifically designed for younger children.

Cookery
Small, table top cookers offer scope for work giving a great deal of pleasure as well as opportunities to experiment and draw conclusions. First-hand experience is gained in weighing, timing, smelling and tasting. Contrasts can be made between hot and cold, wet and dry things, liquids and solids, soluble and insoluble things. Investigations can be made to find out what happens when solids are mixed together, liquids with liquids and when solids are mixed with liquids. Work can be done on the effects of varying components in a basic recipe, e.g. the proportions of ingredients, of adding or leaving out an ingredient, of varying the accepted method of cooking a sponge cake.

6 Topics with science as the central core

In contrast to work on general themes in which the science content is sought and extracted, time can be given to projects with an obvious core of science, and where other areas of the curriculum arise from and support this core.

In our school, these projects are usually spread over half a term. One may follow another directly if there is an obvious connection between the themes. Otherwise, emphasis is placed on another aspect of the curriculum, using a topic where science is subsidiary.

Four examples of such science biased themes are described in terms of how the work was planned for vertically grouped classes of 4 to 7 year old children. The topics included:

1) Feel, touch and texture
2) Feet and shoes
3) Movement—for living and non-living things
4) Flying, floating and spinning in the air

Each followed a set pattern:

1) Class discussion
2) Class experiments
3) Group activity work appropriate to age and ability, evaluation and recording of tests
4) Class discussion

The time allocation was planned to allow a whole morning a week for the experiments. Related language, mathematics and craft work followed from the practical work.

Topic 1 Feel, touch and texture

Week 1
  Class discussion—what do we feel with?
How do we feel things? We feel with our fingers but can we feel with anything else?
  Class experiment
Blindfold children and let them feel objects with other parts of their bodies, e.g. elbows, feet, faces, tongues, etc. Let them describe what they feel. Language is important to describe sensations. Make a list of suitable words. Do the children understand these words?
  Group Activities
Group 1 older or more able children. Writing to describe certain objects by feel only, with no reference to colour or visual appearance. The children can be blindfolded if they wish, to prevent distractions while they 'feel'.
Group 2 middle age group. Working in pairs—one wearing gloves and a blindfold to describe to the other an object and to name it.
Group 3 younger and less able children. Use 'feely' bags. Guess what is inside and try to draw a picture of it.

Week 2
  Class discussion—what do things feel like?
What words can we use to describe the texture of various things? Do the children know what texture means?
  Class experiment
Select one object and several children. Invite each child to use a different word to describe what it feels like. Write down a list of words that describe the object. Talk about opposites, e.g. rough/smooth. What things can be grouped according to their texture?
  Group Activities
Group 1 Explore the possibilities of changing the texture of paper by various means—cutting, sticking, folding, etc.
Group 2 Sort the rag bag and cut out samples of different textured fabrics. A mixed collection of paper can be sorted in the same way, samples cut out and displayed. How would the children describe the different textures of paper and fabric?
Group 3 Look around the classroom and choose rough/smooth or hard/soft objects to make a display table.

Week 3
  Class discussion—how are objects with different textures made?
How is something made smooth or rough? Can we change the texture of an object?

Class experiment
What happens when we rub sandpaper over a rough piece of wood? Try rubbing sandpaper over a smooth piece of fabric. Why does the wood become smooth and the fabric rough? What do the children think?

Group Activities
Group 1 Try to copy the texture of sandpaper by sticking sand on cardboard. Try using salt or sugar. Test the 'sandpapers'—do they work—which sort is best and why?

Group 2 Use drawing pins or cut straws stuck on card to make different textures. Cut small strands of wool and stick them on card so that they overlap, giving a 'pile' effect like carpet.

Group 3 Use Plasticine first for experimenting and then use clay for permanent display. A variety of textures can be made using different tools to create different effects.

Week 4
Class discussion—using and testing textures
Certain textures are made for a specific purpose, e.g. sandpaper for smoothing wood, rubber tread on tyres for gripping the road. What other examples can the children think of? How can these textures be tested to see how well they perform their task? Why should we need to test things?

Group Activities
Group 1 Collect different types of paper and test each one with pencil, ball-point and felt tip pen to see which type of paper is best suited to each medium. Why do some types of paper soak up felt tip ink or paint? Why is it difficult to write on greaseproof paper? Do the children know?

Group 2 Test different types of fabric for wear and strength by rubbing each one twenty times with sandpaper. Are rough textured fabrics stronger than smooth, fine textured ones?

Group 3 Test different grades of sandpaper—rough, medium and fine by rubbing each one twenty times on wood and observing the effects. Does the rough sandpaper last longer than the fine? Which makes the wood smoother?

In all these test situations, it is important that the children realize that the same procedure must be applied to each item to be tested. Results can be recorded in histogram form with written explanations.

The children can write about what they did in any of the activity sessions—this serves to consolidate what they have learnt.

Topic 2 Feet and shoes

Week 1
Class discussion—why do we wear shoes?
Why do we need different kinds of shoes? Make a list of different types of

shoes. Can we wear anyone else's shoes? Does size matter—why? What happens when we go to buy a pair of shoes—fitting and measuring, etc.

Class experiment

Remove one shoe from each girl in the class and mix up these shoes. The girls sit on their other foot, hiding their other shoe. Boys must try to match up the remaining shoes to the correct foot. Ask the girls to say how the shoes felt when tried on their feet. Were they too big or too small, did they feel comfortable or uncomfortable, were they the wrong shape?

Group Activities

Each of the children removes one shoe, places it on a piece of paper and draws around it. The older children measure the outline, both length and width, and write down the measurements. The children can then remove their socks and draw around their feet. Older children again can measure the outline and record to compare the measurements with those of their shoes. The children can colour in both shoes and foot to look like their own and cut them out. Try fitting the foot shape inside the shoe shape. How well does it fit? Is there a gap all round the foot shape? Why should there be a gap? Can we tell how soon anyone will need to have a larger pair of shoes?

The foot and shoe cut-outs can be displayed so that the children can compare their own with their classmates'.

Week 2

Class discussion—testing materials

What are shoes made from? Make a list of different materials that are used to make all the types listed last week. We have different materials for different uses. What qualities must the upper and soles of shoes have? Talk about the properties of leather, rubber, canvas, suede and PVC plastic.

Produce samples of these materials and let the children examine them by feeling, smelling, stretching, etc. and so compare them.

Class experiment

The children can test samples of each one of the materials for properties of water-proofness, warmth, coolness and wear (friction). The results can be recorded on a table with the samples as illustrations.

Week 3

Class discussion—how is a shoe made?

Ask the children for their own ideas—where are shoes made? Explain how shoes used to be made by hand on a *last*—show a last. Lasts are used in factories to press the shoe into the right shape. Demonstrate this with an old shoe. Dismantle it and name all the parts. Count the parts—there are a surprising number. Which bit goes where?

Class experiment

Let the children try to dismantle some old P.E. shoes using scissors and their own strength. How strong are the shoes and what are they made from?

The children can also try to match up mixed pairs of P.E. shoes from an assorted box by judging the size first and then checking the size number inside the shoe. Can they find a pair to fit their own feet? Again they can check the size numbers.

Week 4
Class discussion—making a pair of sandals
Briefly revise from last week how shoes are made and then discuss how we could make some shoes ourselves. Let the children contribute their own ideas, bearing in mind that the class does not have any leather. Where do factories get leather from? What other material could we use? How can we put the shoes together? Factories use special gluing machines to stitch the materials together. What could we use?
Class experiment
Show the children how to make a simple pair of sandals by drawing round their own shoe on a sample of vinyl floor covering. This makes the sole. Then by selecting suitable pieces of fabric from the rag bag, make the criss-cross straps which can be stapled on to the vinyl sole.

Week 5
Class discussion—number work on shoes
Ask the children what sort of number work they think can be investigated in studying shoes. Suggest making pictorial block graphs and histograms about shoe colour, laces, size, etc. What does making a graph involve? What are graphs for? Explain that graphs give us useful information at a glance without us having to read a lot.
Class experiment
Divide the class into three or four groups. Each group is to construct a graph about shoes using a particular feature, e.g. colour, size, with or without laces, different fastenings, etc. as the basis for each graph. Make sure that each child in the group knows what he has to do. For example, in the group making a graph about shoe colour one child could record all the red shoes, another all the black shoes, etc. Explain that we must not duplicate any results if our graph is to give accurate information.
Group Activities
Group 1 With the children working in pairs, let them measure their heights with shoes on, then off. Let them record the results.
Group 2 Ask each to make a stride on paper, drawing round each foot and then measuring the distance between the two feet.
Group 3 Let each count the distance between two points in footsteps, then in strides. If they estimate first they can see how good their judgement is. This can be recorded in pictorial form.
Group 4 This group is to make prints with their shoes and note the

different patterns in the soles of their different shoes. If each child stands in his shoes in a tray in which there is a foam-backed carpet sample and some paint, and then walks across a sheet of paper, a comparison can be made not only of their sole pattern but also of their strides and size of feet.

Handcraft work on this topic can include making plaster cast prints of hands and feet for comparison. These are made by pressing the hand or feet into softened Plasticine or clay. A wall of cardboard is then put round the edge of the clay and plaster of Paris poured in. This is a very sensitive medium which shows individual finger and foot prints. Plaster cast prints such as these are a very good way for children to compare and examine the variety of individual shapes and patterns in their hands and feet.

Associated work in physical education on feet and the different ways we move leads into the next topic.

Topic 3 Movement—for living and non-living things

Week 1
Class discussion—what is movement?
Does everything move? What things move? List some living things and non-living things. Of the living things, groups can be made under the headings of ourselves, animals, birds, fish, reptiles, insects, molluscs and plants.

Do all these living things move in the same way? Why not? Can the children describe how they think they move?

Class experiment
The class can be divided into groups to observe and examine the movement of as many living things as can be obtained. Two or three children should be the maximum number working on each study.

Ourselves Observations can be made of how people move in different situations. The children can observe the rest of the class. Which parts of the body move? Remember eyes and mouths. Which parts do we move the most? Over a set period the group can record the most used parts of the body. If the class were to be observed at playtime, would the results be the same?

Animals A class pet or one that the children have brought in can provide a good study of animal movement as distinct from human movement. How does the animal move? Is it quick or slow? Which parts of its body move?

Birds They can be observed outside the classroom. Their movement can be studied in the same way as for animals.

Fish Goldfish in a tank provide the easiest way of observing the type of movement that fish make. What results from the flick of their tails? What do they use their fins for? Why do they open and close their mouths?

Reptiles It may be difficult to obtain lizards or slow worms for observation, but if it is possible, the co-ordination of right and left leg movements and the sometimes torpid behaviour of lizards could make for very interesting examination and comparison with other animals.

Insects They can be readily collected and studied. Spiders could also be included as examples of creatures with several legs. Do the legs move independently? Does the insect move anything else?

Molluscs Snails, slugs and worms use a special kind of movement as they have no legs. The movement can best be observed by placing the creature on glass and looking at it from underneath.

Plants Plants move or grow very slowly but children can study them over a longer period by marking growth in height. An experiment to show that plants move towards light can be performed by covering some seedlings with a box in which a small hole has been made. Plants on a window sill will also move their leaves towards the sunlight. How long does it take the plant to do this? Plants with tendrils also provide an interesting subject for observation. Which way round do the tendrils move when they curl?

It is important to compare and contrast the observations of movement in all these varied living things. *Why* do living things move?

Week 2

Class discussion—what things move? Do non-living things move?
Can non-living things move? How many can the children think of? Make a list. Do these things move all by themselves or do we have to help them?

Class experiment
The children can examine and compare the movement of different non-living things. Again it is desirable to have only two children investigating any one object.

Clocks Old clocks are preferable so that the children can remove the cover and see the cog wheels inside. How many cog wheels are there—do they all move in the same way? Why are they different sizes? Can they draw some cog wheels? Cog wheels can be made by sticking corrugated card round the rim of a screw top jar lid or round a cheese box. The children can experiment with two or three to see which way round additional wheels will move. Can the children see the hands of the clock moving? Why does one move more quickly than the other? What makes the hands move?

Rocking objects A collection can be made of rocking toys and tockers. What kind of movement is this? Is it always the same? How long does it last? Tockers are designed to rock for a specific time in seconds. Is the initial push to start them off significant? Why? There are various rocking toys the children can make. The simplest is by folding a piece of paper or card in half and cutting the open end into a curve—experiment with the type of curve. A model that will rock in any direction can be made by pressing Plasticine to an eggshell and inserting a pencil or paper cut-out figure into the Plasticine. Differently weighted figures can be made and the effect investigated.

Objects which roll What kinds of objects roll? What shapes does an object have to be in order to roll? Collect together some objects and sort them into two groups of spherical and cylindrical shapes. Try rolling them. What difference in the movement is there between the spherical and the cylindrical shapes? An experiment that will demonstrate the difference is to place a large book on top of a number of identical balls. A round tin lid placed over the balls will first stop them rolling away. Now push the book to make it move. Will it move in any direction? Compare this movement with a similar set-up using toilet roll tubes instead of balls. Will this move in any direction? Why? Explain that this method of moving a heavy object was used before wheels were invented. Make some cardboard wheels and attach them to a box. Put some 'luggage' in the box and try moving it. Is this a better way to move things—why? The children can make rolling 'machines' of their own. A cotton reel 'tank' can provide interesting work in testing how much power is needed from the wound up elastic band to move the cotton reel.

Week 3
 Class discussion—making things move
We have seen that in order for non-living things to move there has to be some force from us to at least start them off. What sort of force do we need to use? In what situations do we push, pull, lift, drop or throw to make something move?
 Class experiment
Collect a variety of objects of different sizes, weights and shapes and let the children try to push, pull, lift, drop or throw each one, with necessary care, to see in which way it is possible to move the object and which is the best way to move it.

Topic 4 Flying, floating and spinning in the air

Week 1
 Class discussion—what is flying?
What sorts of things can fly? Can we fly? What sorts of things do people make that can fly? What makes them fly and stay in the air? What do the children think?
 Class experiment
Show the children how to make a basic paper aeroplane by folding a sheet of paper. Let the children try different designs adding weights to the plane or cutting and folding to change the shape and air flow. Test the planes, measuring the distance that they can fly and comparing the results. Try to establish some basic theories for good paper planes. Do

larger ones fly better than small ones? Do planes with a wide wing span fly more evenly than those with a more streamlined shape? Does weighting the nose of the plane make a difference? By experimenting the children should find out these things for themselves. The appropriate questions at the appropriate time from the teacher should encourage further investigation.

Making kites is another way to investigate man-made flight. The children can experiment with a variety of materials and designs, testing them and recording the results as for paper planes.

It is important for the children to realize that in each situation the test must be a fair one and conditions the same for each plane or kite.

Week 2
Class discussion—floating in the air
Is floating the same as flying? Why? Can the children think of things that they have seen floating in the air? What sorts of things will float? What makes them float and why do they eventually come down? Explain that the air which we are not able to see but can feel, helps certain objects to float if they are the right sort of shape and weight. Demonstrate with two pieces of paper—one screwed up into a ball and the other flat. Drop them both from the same height. The children should be able to see that the shape is very important, but why does the flat piece float? What do the children think?

Class experiment
Let the children experiment with a variety of objects around the classroom to see what floats and what does not float. They can list these.

The children can then make some floating objects of their own. Shuttlecocks can be made by sticking feathers into a cork. Let them find out for themselves where the feather should be positioned for the best results. Parachutes can be made using different types of fabric with string tied at the corners and joined to a weight. Is the weight an important factor—how heavy must it be? Is the length of the strings important? Does making a hole in the top of the parachute fabric make any difference?

Week 3
Class discussion—spinning in the air and using air to move things
What sorts of things move or spin in the air? Windmills are a good example of this. How does the air make them move? Can we feel the air when it moves things? Let the children blow onto their hands to feel air moving. We call moving air wind. On a windy day what sorts of things have the children seen that are blowing about? How strong can the wind be? Talk about storms and hurricanes.

Class experiment
Let the children try using air by waving pieces of card. Let them make some paper fans. Can they use these to make the air move other things?

Try fanning some paper 'fish' across the floor. Let the children make some kites using a variety of materials and designs. Polystyrene tiles are good for this. What effect does the tail of a kite have? Can the children see that the tail helps to balance its flight in the air? A bird's tail helps to balance its flight. Many animals use their tails to balance their movement. Can the children see that when man makes something, he tends to copy nature in many ways?

What kinds of natural things spin in the air? Collect some sycamore seeds and watch them spin. Let the children make their own paper spinner. A rectangle of paper is cut lengthwise about half way along. The two flaps are folded in opposite directions. A paper clip makes a good weight to balance it. It will spin in a very satisfactory way on dropping. Do the children know why it spins? Let them suggest their own reasons.

Show the children how to make a paper windmill. Try blowing it to make it spin. Does it matter where you blow? Take the windmills outside on a breezy day. Is the wind outside better at blowing the windmills than our breath?

Let the children write about their experiments. The failures are just as important as the successes in scientific investigations.

Conclusions

Science for infants uses their natural curiosity and gives purpose to their basic learning. Situations already exist in infant classes which lend themselves to the development of thinking in an ordered and therefore scientific manner.

Science can be incorporated into topics across the curriculum or it can provide the central theme using language, mathematics and craft work to describe and evaluate the work done.

In planning the learning situations, one must provide experience which will lead to a development of skills, the formation of basic concepts and the promotion of scientific attitudes and methods.

References

References

Chapter One
1 Department of Education and Science, *Primary Education in England: A Survey by H.M. Inspectors of Schools*, HMSO, 1978.
2 Department of Education and Science, Assessment of Performance Unit, *Science in Schools—Age 11*, Report no. 1, HMSO, 1981.

Chapter Three
1 The Schools Council, 'Time Stages 1 & 2', *Science 5-13*, Macdonald Educational, 1972.
2 Department of Education and Science, *Primary Education in England: A Survey by H.M. Inspectors of Schools*, HMSO, 1978.

Chapter Five
1 RSPCA, *Animals in Schools*, RSPCA, Horsham, Sussex.

Chapter Six
1 The Schools Council, *The School Outdoor Resource Area*, Longman.
2 The Schools Council, 'Minibeasts Stages 1 & 2', *Science 5-13*, Macdonald Educational, 1972.
3 The Nuffield Foundation, *Junior Science Source Book: Animals and Plants*, Collins, 1967.
4 Lynn, Veronica, 'Microbes and Man', *Science in Focus*, Evans.
5 May, John, 'The Balance of Nature', *Science in Focus*, Evans.
6 The Schools Council, 'Trees Stages 1 & 2', *Science 5-13*, Macdonald Educational, 1972.
7 The Schools Council, 'Working with Wood Background Information and Stages 1 & 2', *Science 5-13*, Macdonald Educational, 1972.
8 Diamond, Dorothy, *Science From Wood* (Teaching Primary Science series), Macdonald Educational.
9 The Schools Council, 'Using the Environment Investigations Part 2', *Science 5-13*, Macdonald Educational, 1972.
10 Hooper, Ted, *Guide to Bees and Honey*, Blandford Press.
11 The General Secretary, *British Beekeepers Association*, High Trees, Dean Lane, Mersham, Surrey, RH1 3AH.
12 The British Waterfowl Association, *Save the Village Pond*, The British Waterfowl Association, Bell House, 111-113 Lambeth Road, London SE2.
13 Dyson, John, *The Pond Book*, Puffin Books.
14 Channell, Jim, *Life in Ponds*, Frederick Warne (Publishers) Ltd.